# INQUIRE

## Suggested Activities to Motivate the
## Teaching of Intermediate Science

AUTHOR
**EDUCATIONAL SERVICE, INC.**
EDITED BY
**John M. Youngpeter**
ILLUSTRATED BY
**Dennis P. Davan**

PUBLISHED BY
**EDUCATIONAL SERVICE, INC.**
P.O. Box 219
Stevensville, Michigan 49127

# TABLE OF CONTENTS

## SECTION IV: "WEATHER"

## SECTION V: "EARTH SCIENCE"

## SECTION VI: "LIGHT — HEAT"

## CHAPTER 1: LIGHT

## CHAPTER 2: HEAT

# INTRODUCTION

INQUIRE, a SPICE series publication by Educational Service, Inc., is designed to meet the needs within the area of intermediate science, 4-8. (PROBE, primary science activities, is available for grades K-4.) Each activity in INQUIRE includes a description of all necessary materials and preparations and an example of exactly how each project may be presented to your group. Activities and ideas are presented in the areas of simple machines, flight and space, weather, earth science, light and heat, sound, electricity and magnetism and the animal kingdom in order to stimulate the students to examine the known and dig beneath the surface of the unknown.

Intermediate science is not a subject apart from other subject matter but is a unification of all subjects and attitudes which we wish to instill and develop in children. Discovering nails in the alley while working with magnets is the ideal time to work on community pride and citizen welfare. Courtesy can be taught naturally when using the telephone as an experiment in sound. Each activity and experiment has value far beyond the learning of a scientific fact or principle.

It is hoped that you will view the ideas you find in INQUIRE as a basis for activities you can develop to meet the individual needs of each of your students. Herein lies the teacher's response when a child's expression demands, "Teach me."

# SECTION I:
## "Basic Scientific Skills"

## *1. THE EFFECTS OF MAGNIFIED SUNLIGHT (Grades 4-8)

**A. Purpose:** To increase variety and accuracy in observation.

**B. Materials:** Sunlight, magnifying glasses, paper and pencils.

**C. Introduction to the Class:** I have a magnifying glass, does everyone know how a magnifying glass works? Today, we are going to do an experiment showing how the power of sunlight through the use of a magnifying glass will burn paper. After I demonstrate, we will divide into groups (have one magnifying glass and enough paper for each group) and each group will conduct their own experiment. Before we begin our experiment, I would like each of you to record on paper the following things; the size, color and texture of the paper. Record the changes that are taking place during and after the experiment.

**D. Variation:** Instead of paper, use cloth, plastic or fruit. Let each group take a different item and record their findings as in previous experiments. After all experiments are completed, let each group present their own findings to the class.


## 2. DISCOVERING NATURE THROUGH OBSERVATION (Grades 4-8)

**A. Purpose:** To increase the observation of nature in your local area.

**B. Materials:** Each student will need a notebook in which their observations can be

*This activity is available in Inquire Volume I of the Spice™ Duplicating Masters.

recorded. You may also divide the class into groups of threes or fours for recording purposes.

**C. Procedure:** Take the class through a particular area near school and have them list the various items of nature they see. When you return, list on the board all items that were seen. Allow students to note the difference between what they had seen and what the class as a total saw.

**D. Variation:** The class may investigate further into specific groups; such as, How many different types of trees were seen? How many different plants, soils, etc., were seen?

## 3. GET A CLOSER LOOK (Grades 4-5)

**A. Purpose:** To introduce the use of magnification with a hand lens and a microscope or microprojector.

**B. Materials:** Hand lenses or reading glass.

**C. Introduction to the Class:** When we use a lens, we can see small parts of things which are not possible to see without it. The shape of the lens gathers the light coming from the object and brings it to the eye so that the object seems to be bigger. Is the actual size of the object changed? (Students may use the lenses to look at a newsprint. By moving the lens aside they can see that the letters have not been changed in size, but only look like they have.) Look at many things; such as, your hand, the table surface and other things around the classroom. The thicker the lens is, the bigger it makes the object under it appear. Try it after putting 2 lenses together. That is how a microscope is made. Does it make the objects even bigger with 2 lenses?

**D. Variation:** Make a lens with a drop of water. Place a drop of water on a glass microscope slide or on a piece of transparent plastic which is stiff enough to support the weight of the drop. (A drop of transparent glue or clear Karo syrup also works very well.) For materials to study, use sandpaper, steel wool, newsprint, cloth of various colors and textures. Binoculars may also be used as a magnifier of close objects. Place your eye near the lens of the small end and bring the object to be viewed close to the eyepiece, being certain that there is enough light shining on the object being viewed so that it can be clearly seen. Move the binoculars back and forth to bring the object into focus.

## 4. EVERY PICTURE TELLS A STORY (Grades 4-6)

**A. Purpose:** To provide information from which inferences can be drawn.

**B. Materials:** Overhead transparencies or posters.

**C. Preparation:** The pictures may be from magazines providing a basis for inferring; such as, an animal resting in the shade, not the sunshine; sketches of part of an animal projecting from behind a building; or footprint sketches showing, for example, the footprints of a person, dog and rabbit in a design implying action.

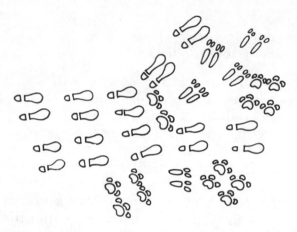

**D. Introduction to the Class:** I am going to project on the screen a picture (or show a poster). What would you say happened here if you were a detective? (It may be necessary to have some questions which will help the class get started.) Answers should be accepted that are logical for the kind of data provided. There is no right answer, only logical ones.

**E. Variation:** Once the class understands the nature of such inferences, they can draw their own transparency sheets for projecting. They may also wish to collect magazine pictures which can be used in the same way.

## 5. CLASSIFYING PEANUTS (Grades 4-8)

**A. Purpose:** To permit students to develop systems of classification and realize how arbitrary these systems are. Also, powers of observation are enhanced.

**B. Materials:** Peanuts in the shells (enough for each student or each group of students to have 5 or 6 peanuts), paper cups in which to dispense them.

**C. Introduction to the Class:** Classifying is a means of filing things or facts. Words in a dictionary are "classified" in an alphabetical way. The names in a phone book are classified in the same way. As soon as you know the system, you can use it easily. Notes in your notebooks are "classified" according to subjects probably so you can find information when you want it. Animals and plants are classified by scientists who study them. They are classified according to certain characteristics they have. We are going to set up a classification system for peanuts. Work in groups (of 2 or 3). Get a cup of peanuts and decide how many ways you can classify them. What characteristics about the nuts can be used to classify them? Make a list of your ideas and we will list these on the board when you have finished. (After 10 minutes or so have students give the ways they think the nuts can be classified. Ask the class which ways are the best? Hopefully, they will agree that the most consistent and most obvious points are easiest to use. Size, shape, color, texture, number of cells, etc.)

**D. Variation:** Objects can be gathered in the classroom for a classification exercise. Or, use a collection of nails, screws, staples and bolts. These can be placed in plastic bags so that each group has the same objects. If this grouping is used, they can be projected in an outline by using the overhead projector. After the class has set up their own systems, project a set of the objects and use them as a class discussion is held.

# *6. MEASURING THE HEIGHT OF A TREE (Grades 4-8)

**A. Purpose:** To introduce an indirect way of measuring.

**B. Materials:** A tree on the school grounds (on a sunny day).

**C. Introduction to the Class:** How can you determine how high a tree is without measuring it with a measuring stick? Yes, it is possible. One way to determine its height is to measure the tree's shadow and then measure the shadow of any short object that is standing erect; such as, a post, a man, etc. Suppose a six-foot man casts a shadow that is 10 feet long and the tree's shadow is seventy feet long. By using a proportion the tree's height can be measured. For example, using the tree shadow of seventy feet and the 6-foot man's shadow of 10 feet, the proportion will be:

$$\text{then,} \quad 10 : 6 : : 70 : X$$
$$6 \text{ x } 70 : : 10 \text{ x } X$$
$$\text{then,} \quad \frac{6 \text{ x } 70}{10} : : X$$
$$\text{then,} \quad 42 : : X$$

The tree is 42 feet high.

# 7. DETERMINING THE RATE OF THE PULSE (Grades 4-8)

**A. Purpose:** To determine the rate of events occurring over a given period of time.

**B. Materials:** A clock with a second hand or a watch.

*This activity is available in Inquire Volume I of the Spice™ Duplicating Masters.

**C. Introduction to the Class:** To decide on the rate that some events occur, what must we know? That is, how fast a car goes is determined how? (Discussion — by knowing distance covered and rate of time required to do it.) One common rate is the rate of the pulse. Who knows what the pulse is? (Discussion — the number of beats the heart makes in a given period of time.) Can everyone find his pulse? Find it either below the "angle of the jaw" on your neck or on the wrist. To determine this rate, what information must we have? (Number of beats or pumps in a given period of time. Commonly, the rate is beats per minute. Have students count for ½ minute and multiply by 2, or count for 60 seconds.)

**D. Variation:** Modifications, after the idea of rate is understood, can be comparing girls to boys rates before and after running up and down stairs, etc. Graphing can be used here to record and compare results.

# SECTION II:
## "Simple Machines"

## Additional Teacher Information

Within PROBE, our primary science hand-book, a machine was defined as a device which increases or magnifies the effort put into work. The six simple machines are: (1) the lever; (2) the pulley; (3) the wheel and axle; (4) the inclined plane; (5) the wedge; and (6) the screw. Illustrations of the three classes of levers are shown below:

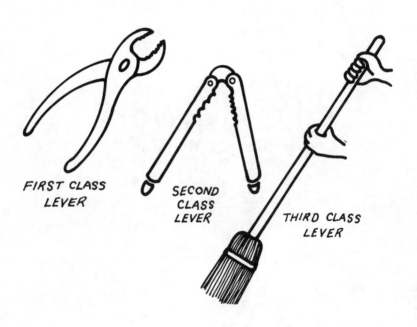

FIRST CLASS LEVER

SECOND CLASS LEVER

THIRD CLASS LEVER

# 1. SIMPLE MACHINE BULLETIN BOARD DISPLAY (Grades 4-8)

**A. Purpose:** To illustrate and give understanding of simple machines.

**B. Materials:** Pictorial magazines and scissors.

**C. Introduction to the Class:** How many machines did you see on the way to school today? What types of machines were they? Do you know the various classes of machines?

There are six simple machines into which all machines fall regardless of complexity. The six simple machines are:

1. the lever
2. the pulley
3. the wheel and axle
4. the inclined plane
5. the wedge
6. the screw

We are going to create a bulletin board display of various types of machines. As you find a picture of a machine from the magazines you have brought, identify the classification of the machine, notice the type of work it does and how it helps our lives. We will divide our bulletin board into seven sections. One section for each class of machine and one section for machines that are a combination of the classes of machines.

**D. Variation:** A bulletin board may be made for weather, heat, sound, electricity, animal and plant life, or earth science. All areas of science lend themselves to the creation of bulletin boards.

# *2. SCIENCE DETECTIVES (Grades 4-6)

**A. Purpose:** To learn to identify and describe simple machines.

**B. Materials:** A list of machines that fall into the category of the simple machine; pulley, lever, wheel and axle, wedge, screw and inclined plane.

**C. Introduction to the Class:** We are going to pretend that we are detectives in search of some very important articles. We will divide into two teams. Each team will need a **Chief of Detectives** and the rest of the team will be investigators. Each team will decide upon a machine that will be their most wanted article, then make up ten clues that will help identify the machine. I will help you so you are not both searching for the same object.

The Chief of the first team will read the first clue. If the other team of detectives can guess the machine on the first clue, they score 100 points. (Be sure to talk over your answer before you call out.) Each clue takes ten points off the score. If it takes all ten clues, then the score will be zero. The team of detectives with the highest score will win the game.

Are you ready? Decide on your machine and make up your clues. Which team will be the best detectives?

(The teacher should help each team choose clues that will be pertinent to the study area. Example: This machine is a lever used on a farm.)

**D. Correlation:** This game can be played using health and safety facts, the elements, minerals, social studies or language arts. The

*This activity is available in Inquire Volume I of the Spice™ Duplicating Masters.

teacher will be able to incorporate this game into many subject areas.

## 3. FOOTBALL GAME (Grades 4-6)

**A. Purpose:** To strengthen vocabulary used in the science of simple machines.

**B. Preparation:** Place the vocabulary used in the study of simple machines on the chalkboard or on flashcards.

**C. Introduction to the Class:** Let's play a game of football. Who knows how many points are scored for a touchdown? Six is right. In our game, the team making a touchdown also scores six points. We will have two teams. (Select teams.) The team that gets the most points will win the football game!

We are not going to play with a football. We are going to play with words. On these cards, I have words that we have been using in our work on machines. When I hold up a card, you are to say the word. Each of you will have a chance to name six words. If you name them all correctly, you score a touchdown and your team gets six points. We will draw straws to see which team starts. When each member of both teams has had a chance to name the words, the game will be over and we will count the scores. We will need a scorekeeper for each team. Who will volunteer for that job? I will hold the cards up one at a time and you name them as quickly as you can.

We will score a little differently than in football, because you can still make points for your team even if you do not make a touchdown. You will be able to score one point for each word that you name correctly. Are you ready to start the game?

**Example of word list:** machine, lever, fulcrum, wheel, axle, springs, weights, etc.

**D. Variation:** The game may be played by letting a child point to the words on the board or by putting the words in a pocket chart and each team member drawing his list of words.

**Football** may be played by two children at a time who draw their words from the pocket chart and play the game after completion of some stated work.

**E. Correlation: Football** can be used as a word-drill game in connection with any unit of work. Knowledge of words needed for the proposed work will be the goal of the drill.

## 4. MACHINE SCAVENGER HUNT
(Grades 4-6)

**A. Purpose:** To activate interest in machines and the work they do; to promote group work.

**B. Preparation:** Prepare a list of items which demonstrate different kinds of machines and the work they do. Make enough copies to give one to each group of five children in class. These lists should not be the same.

**Example:**

1. Find a picture of a lever used to work on a car.

2. Find a machine that helps in house cleaning. If you cannot bring it to school, draw a picture of it and tell where it was and what work it was doing.

3. Find a picture of an inclined plane doing work.

4. Find a picture of the machine used to clean snow from the sidewalk. Be able to tell what kind of machine it is.

**C. Introduction to the Class:** What is a scavenger hunt? (If some of the children do not know, explain it to them.) Would you like to go on a scavenger hunt? Can you work together for a little while after school? I will select one person, then he will pick four others to work with him on the hunt. This is not a contest, because I hope every group will come back to school with all of their items.

Tomorrow morning during sharing time, we shall show and tell what we have been able to find.

Here are your lists of machines. Have fun finding them!

**D. Variation:** This could be used to find machines at school. Example: pencil sharpener, broom, shovel, etc.

**E. Correlation:** A scavenger hunt of this type could be used in different areas of science; such as, plants, animals, rocks, etc. This could also be used in social studies work by finding articles at home and in the community, giving more time to find the materials. The work could be done entirely at school by using only magazine pictures.

## 5. IN MY HOUSE (Grades 4-6)

**A. Purpose:** To broaden the concept of machines and their uses through discovering what machines Mother and Father use, the work of the machines and how they help the parent.

**B. Preparation:** Place on the chalkboard or chart, a list of activities that a child might choose to report his findings to the group. A chart is preferable because it can be left hanging indefinitely.

The list might include:

1. Make a chart showing machines used in a particular type of work.

2. Make models of machines and tell how they are used.

3. Draw pictures showing Mother or Father working with a machine and write a story of your discovery to go with your picture.

4. Take photos of a job being done with machines.

5. Tell how Mother and Father use many different machines to help make your home a better place to live.

**C. Introduction to the Class:** We have talked about some of the interesting things your parents do in which they use machines. We use machines in practically everything we do. We are called a nation of machines. It would be fun to have an exhibit showing how our parents use machines. In order to have an exhibit, we will have to decide upon a way of showing what we discover. You will want to observe and ask questions so that your report will be worthwhile to others as well as to yourself.

I have put on this chart a list of different ways to show what you have discovered. You may think of a much better way to show your work than one of my suggestions. If we decide to have this exhibit, we could invite other classes and our parents to come and see what we have discovered. We might have an "open house" such as P.T.A. has. How many of you would like to work on a show of machines and their work? Think this over, and tomorrow be ready to tell me what you want to work on.

(This project should be carried on for about three or four weeks and culminate in an open house for parents and schoolmates that would last for an hour or so. Invitations should be sent to those interested.)

**D. Variation:** Parents and relatives may help the child find many interesting aspects of machine science. The exhibit could show any scientific principle involved in work. Mother and child might make a sampling of foods that contain acid. Father might work with the child to mix and pour cement.

This exhibit might be displayed at the city library or in a store show window. The people in the community are glad to show the work of children to the public.

**E. Correlation:** An exhibit might be made for economics or social studies. This is a perfect medium to display health and safety concepts.

## 6. SPOT IT (Grades 4-5)

**A. Purpose:** To help the child observe more carefully.

**B. Materials:** A picture from a magazine, mounted on the bulletin board, a large envelope labeled **"answers,"** fastened near the picture.

**C. Introduction to the Class:** Today, I have put on the bulletin board a picture with many different kinds of machines in it. During the day, I want you to study this picture very carefully. We will see just how well you really look at things. You are to discover the simple machines that are in the picture and tell what work each one is doing. When you have your answers ready, put your name on your paper and put it in this big envelope marked **answers.**

Tomorrow, we shall look at the answers and discuss the picture and the objects you found in it. Remember to look very carefully before you try to answer.

**D. Variation:** Use pictures to illustrate living things, non-living things, how air is being used (breathing, pumping up a tire, etc.).

**E. Correlation:** This game can be used in many subject areas; such as, social studies, health, economics, etc., with the result that the child will be trained to actually see what he is looking at.

## 7. FIND YOUR FAMILY (Grades 4-6)

**A. Purpose:** To strengthen knowledge of kinds of simple machines; to check for those who need help and those who know the subject well.

**B. Materials:** A card for each child with the name or picture of a machine on it. Each machine should represent a lever, a pulley, a wedge, a screw, a wheel and axle, or an inclined plane. Pictures can be cut from magazines or drawn in a simple manner by the teacher.

**C. Introduction to the Class:** We are going to play a game called Find Your Family. What kinds of simple machines do we have? That's right; the lever, the pulley, the wedge, the screw, the wheel and axle and the inclined plane. Each of you will be a machine in this game. I will give you a card that tells you what machine you are. Each of these machines will belong in the family of one of the simple machines. You will have to figure out to what family you belong.

When I call, "Find Your Family," you will look for other machines that fall into the same group as your own machine. Would the bicycle and the scooter be in the same family? Yes, they would. When you find a member of your family, join hands. As soon as I call out, turn your cards face out so everyone can see what machine you are. I will count to ten slowly. If you have not found your family by then, perhaps the rest of your family will find you. Let's try it once to be sure that you know how to play the game.

We will change cards after each game so you will be a different machine each time we play. Are you ready?

**D. Variation:** This game can be used in general science with plants, animals, minerals, etc. The game will help the slow learner categorize the different types of objects used.

**E. Correlation:** Find Your Family can be a good language arts game.

## 8. MACHINE RELAY (Grades 4-6)

**A. Purpose:** To review examples of machines.

**B. Materials:** Use two sections of the chalkboard. Divide each section into six parts. Label each with a class of machine.

| Lever | Pulley | Inclined Plane | Screw | Wedge | Wheel and Axle |
|---|---|---|---|---|---|
| | | | | | |

**C. Introduction to the Class:** I have made two charts on the chalkboard with the names of the kinds of simple machines on them. Both charts are exactly alike. Tell me the names of the machine types when I point to them.

We are going to play a game with these charts. This will be a relay game. Each team will line up behind the captain and when I say "go," each captain will go to the board and write the name of a machine under the right heading. He will hurry back, hand the chalk to the next in line and then go to the end of his line. The next child will now go to the board and write the name of a different machine under the right heading and then do as the captain did. Go as fast as you can, but write so that we can read what you have written. You must not run. When either captain gets back to the first of his line with the chalk in his hand, the game is over.

(Select two captains and let them choose children for their teams.)

We will check the lists. One point will be taken off the score for each mistake made, so the team to finish first might not be the real winner. Do not hurry so fast to finish that you make a mistake. Each right answer scores one point. Are you ready?

**D. Correlation:** This type of relay may be used in the study of plants, animals, constellations, minerals, etc. The teacher will be able to devise many different headings.

## 9. USE IT WELL (Grades 4-6)

**A. Purpose:** To review ways in which we use each kind of simple machine.

**B. Materials:** Strips of paper with names of machines on them.

**C. Introduction to the Class:** We are going to have fun today. We are going to play a game that is something like charades except we shall be guessing the whole answer instead of parts of it. We shall divide into teams of six members. Each team will get a chance to act out the use of a machine. I shall give each team a slip of paper on which is given the name of the machine that you will be using. As the actor for the team plays his part, the rest of the teams try to guess the machine he is using and what the machine is doing. As soon as a team thinks they know, call out the answer because the first team to guess correctly will score ten points.

Each team will have one turn and the team with the highest score wins for today. Here are your first slips. Keep the machine a secret from the other teams until it is your turn to act.

**D. Variations:** Use It Well may be played by two or three children instead of a team. To make this a silent game to be used while others are working, the answers may be written.

**E. Correlation:** Play-acting is always a good way to show uses of things or an emotional reaction to a situation.

# *10. SCIENTIST OF THE WEEK
(Grades 4-8)

**A. Purpose:** To review the uses of the pulley.

**B. Materials:** For each student: pencil and notebook paper, drawing paper and crayons.

**C. Introduction to the Class:** Different organizations pick the most outstanding person of the year. The movie people pick out the best actor, comedian, etc. We often hear of the "Play of the Week" or the "Book of the Month." Our room is going to pick the "Scientist Of The Week." We are going to have a little contest each week. I shall give you a topic to work on and you will write a short story about this topic and draw a picture to illustrate your story. I shall select the three that I believe to be the best and put them on the bulletin board. You will not put your names on your papers, because the whole class will pick out the "Scientist Of The Week." Each of you will look at the work very carefully and Monday we will vote to find out which one you think is best. The one that the class picks will be displayed all week, headed: **The Scientist Of The Week.** After we have made our final selection, the person to whom the work belongs will put his name under it so we will all know who is doing such fine work.

We are going to start gathering material for our first contest entry right now. This is our topic (write on the board) **How We Use The Pulley.** Take your time to think and work so you can be proud of your entry.

*This activity is available in Inquire Volume I of the Spice™ Duplicating Masters.

**D. Variation:** Older children may be given topics that need research as well as review. Younger children may use this contest and draw pictures only.

**E. Correlation:** A contest of this type correlates with all topics of study whether in science or in other areas. The "Author of the Week" can be selected, the "Mathematician of the Week," etc.

## 11. TOOL MAKING (Grades 6-8)

**A. Purpose:** To strengthen the concept that simple machines are the tools with which we work; to make a useful tool that is needed for other science work.

**B. Materials:** To make a dissecting tool — pencil; rubber band or thread; a long, slender, dressmaking pin. To make science forceps — small brads; elastic band; two slender pieces of wood about seven inches long and three-eighths of an inch wide; a block or cardboard layers one-eighth of an inch thick.

**C. Introduction to the Class:** We have been talking about useful machines and I wondered if you would like to make two tools that we need for use in some of our other science work. I should like two volunteer committees to work on a dissecting tool and some forceps. While you are making the tools, determine how they will be used and under what class of machines they fall. Who would like to volunteer for this work? (Select two committees of not more than five members. These children will work together while the rest of the class proceeds with other work. Have the following directions made out on a card to be given to the chairman of each committee. Let the committee bring in their own materials for their project.)

## Directions for Dissecting Tool

Use a long, slender, dressmaking pin. Use a rubber band or thread to fasten or bind the pin tightly to a pencil or dowel for half the length of the pin.

## Directions for Science Forceps

Use two slender pieces of wood about seven inches long and three-eighths of an inch wide. Taper one end of each stick to a blunt point, making filed grooves on the inside to provide a better grip.

Insert a small block or cardboard layers one-eighth of an inch thick about an inch down from the top or end without grooves. Fasten with small brads. Bind the top ends with a strong elastic band.

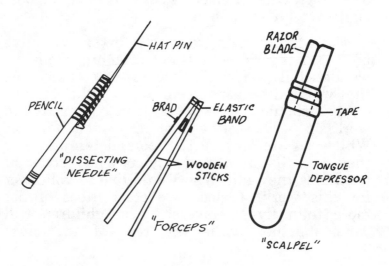

## Use of the Dissecting Tool

Use this tool when dissecting birds, insects, small animals or flowers.

## Use of the Science Forceps

Use the forceps for feeding terrarium inhabitants or to lift small objects from water or jars.

**D. Variation:** You can also make a scalpel such as the one shown in the illustration.

# SECTION III:
## "Flight And Space"

# *1. NEIGHBORS IN SPACE (Grades 4-8)

**A. Purpose:** To learn of the planets and their position in relation to other planets; to learn that each moves in a certain path around the sun.

**B. Materials:** Black crayon, drawing paper, white chalk.

**C. Preparation:** Draw a circle on the floor in the center of the classroom for the sun.

**D. Introduction to the Class:** Today, we are going to play that we are our neighbors in space, the planets. Each of you will have a chance to observe how the planets move and to follow the orbit of a planet.

First, we will have to make name cards so everyone will know what planet we represent. (The teacher selects a child for the sun and nine children for the planets. Try to select children according to the size of the planet. Each child writes on the drawing paper with the black crayon the name of the planet he is to represent and pins it on.)

The sun, our largest star, will stand here in the center of the circle I have drawn on the floor. The sun does not move.

(The teacher will draw a circle around the sun and place the child who is Mercury on this line. Draw a second circle for Venus. Continue to draw a circle and place the child who is to be a planet on the correct circle. Each circle is the orbit of that particular planet. Draw circles and place planets as the diagram indicates.)

Now, boys and girls, we have the planets placed in their correct position to the sun. Each planet moves around the sun. The circles I have

—31—

*This activity is available in Inquire Volume I of the Spice™ Duplicating Masters.

drawn show the path each planet takes. Remember the sun stands still. Are the planets ready to start moving in their orbits? Now, all nine planets start to move around the sun.

Watch closely! It will soon be your turn to pretend that you are a planet.

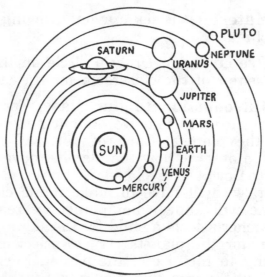

**E. Variation:** Add a moon child as the earth's satellite. Send children into orbit as Sputnik, Explorer, Vanguard, Echo, or Friendship 7 as new neighbors in space. Smaller children may be added as other moons or satellites around other planets. Let different children represent the planets while the first group watches.

**F. Correlation:** Use this activity in discussion of present-day space activities. This can be adapted for use in the study of weather and heat. Distances from the sun and actual time taken to orbit the sun by different planets can be used in number computations with older children.

## 2. PROVE IT! (Grades 4-8)

**A. Purpose:** To motivate independent research.

**B. Materials:** Statements concerning planets, star groups, rockets or jets to be placed on the bulletin board daily.

**C. Introduction to the Class:** We have discussed many interesting phases of space and how we are preparing for space travel. Everyday for two weeks, I am going to put a statement or an article concerning space on the bulletin board. Read each of them carefully and see if you can prove my statement true or show proof that it is false. I may try to trick you by putting statements up that have no scientific basis. If I trick you, I shall win the game. You will have to use your reference books for information, as well as inquiry. This is a research problem that will be entirely your own. Let's see who will come up with the best results from your research.

(The teacher should remind and motivate students everyday until the class swings into the competitive attitude. When this is accomplished, a simple reminder or the placing of the item on the bulletin board when the class is watching will be sufficient to start the group searching.)

**Example of Statement:** A jet passenger plane ascended into the east-west jet stream and proceeded west to California using much less fuel than a lower flight uses. (True)

**D. Variation:** Items may be cut from the newspaper and displayed. Pictures and cartoons may serve to provoke the students into action.

**E. Correlation:** Bulletin board statements may be used for language arts and social studies. Problems can be used in this manner and the children can prove that they have been solved correctly or incorrectly. This type of activity can be used during work on earth science, weather, machines, animals, plants, electricity, sound, light and heat.

## *3. SIZE AND DISTANCE (Grades 6-8)

**A. Purpose:** To make the size and distance of the planets from the sun more meaningful to students.

**B. Materials:** A strip of white mural paper 20 inches wide and 17 feet long. A chart of planet size and distance placed in the classroom where all may study it. Paper and paint.

Place the mural paper in a place where several children can work on it at the same time. Draw a slightly curved line at the left edge of the paper to represent the sun's rim.

**Chart:**

| Planet | Mean Diameter | Average Miles from the Sun |
|---|---|---|
| Mercury | 2,995 miles | 36 million miles |
| Venus | 7,586 miles | 67 million miles |
| Earth | 7,912 miles | 93 million miles |
| Mars | 4,192 miles | 142 million miles |
| Jupiter | 87,842 miles | 484 million miles |
| Saturn | 71,870 miles | 885 million miles |
| Uranus | 29,447 miles | 1,789 million miles |
| Neptune | 29,463 miles | 2,809 million miles |
| Pluto | 3,693 miles | 3,685 million miles |

**C. Introduction to the Class:** We have talked about the size of the planets and how far each one is from the sun. Our chart of planet size and distance has been up for several days

*This activity is available in Inquire Volume I of the Spice™ Duplicating Masters.

and I know many of you have been studying and discussing it. Today, we are going to start using this information to help us really understand what these figures mean. Big figures are fun to know, but we should know what they mean. You can surprise your mother when you go home by telling her something about the size of our planets and how far away from the sun they are. We are going to make a mural of the planets that will give us the exact information that is on this chart.

We will divide into two groups and each group will take half of the planets to work with. We will make the planets and place them on the picture to the exact scale. Of course, our planets cannot be the actual size, can they? The distance and the size will correspond but they will be scaled down to the proper size for our picture. (Divide the class into two groups and give each group the materials needed.)

I'm going to place a chart, beside our chart of actual planet size and distance. This chart shows the size of the planets and the distance we will have to place each from the sun. (Place the chart from page 35 beside the first chart.)

Each planet must be measured and placed in the exact position. Are you ready to start working? Good, here's the information you will need.

## Chart:

| Planet | Size of circle on picture chart | Distance from center of planet to the sun for chart picture |
|---|---|---|
| Mercury | .29 inch | 1.80 inches |
| Venus | .75 inch | 3.35 inches |
| Earth | .79 inch | 4.65 inches |
| Mars | .41 inch | 7.10 inches |
| Jupiter | 8.78 inches | 24.20 inches |
| Saturn | 7.18 inches | 44.25 inches |
| Uranus | 2.94 inches | 89.45 inches |
| Neptune | 2.96 inches | 140.45 inches |
| Pluto | .36 inch | 184.25 inches |

**D. Variation:** When using this activity with slow groups, the teacher and the whole class should work together with the teacher directing.

**E. Correlation:** This chart picture can be used in connection with story writing. The figures and the scale can be used with advanced groups as an arithmetic project.

## *4. DO YOU KNOW ME? (Grades 4-6)

**A. Purpose:** To promote correct spelling of "space" vocabulary; to review factual material learned during the study of Space.

**B. Materials:** A list of factual statements placed on the chalkboard or duplicated for each child. The duplicated sheet is the most successful. Place a list of answers on the board, jumbled and mixed up. If a duplicated sheet is used, these answers will be at the bottom of the sheet.
**Example:** Statement: — This planet has rings. Answer: — (jumbled) Nstaur — Saturn

**C. Introduction to the Class:** I have a puzzle for you. I am going to give you a sheet which has true statements on it about the planets and the constellations. At the bottom of the sheet, you will find the answer but they will be mixed up. You will have to find the right answers and then straighten the letters out so that the words are spelled correctly. The letters will all be there, but you will have to rearrange them in order to have the answer spelled correctly. This is just like a jigsaw puzzle only we will have to put letters together to spell words instead of putting pieces together to make a picture.

—36—

As soon as you receive your sheet, you may start working. See how many of these jumbled words you can straighten out. (Pass out the sheets.)

**D. Variation:** Do You Know Me may be used as a team game. The jumbled words will be on the board and the teams will take turns picking out the right jumbled words to match an oral statement given by the teacher.

**E. Correlation:** Jumbled names of scientists, plants, or animals may be used in place of planets. Spelling words may be used in this manner as an individual game.

## *5. SPACE BASEBALL (Grades 4-8)

**A. Purpose:** To review factual material covered in the study of Space.

**B. Materials:** Prepare four sets of questions about space. Set I consists of easy questions. Sets II, III and IV graduate in difficulty. Set I is put in a box labeled, One-base Hit. Set II is place in a box labeled, Two-base Hit. Set III is put in a box labeled, Three-base Hit. Set IV, the most difficult, is placed in a box labeled, Home Run.

**Examples of questions:**
Set I. Name our largest star. (Sun)
Set II. Why is the earth a planet instead of a star? (It does not produce its own light.)
Set III. What body does the earth and the moon orbit and how long does it take each to complete its orbit? (The earth orbits the sun in 365 days. The moon orbits the earth in 28 days.)

*This activity is available in Inquire Volume I of the Spice™ Duplicating Masters.

Set IV. Name six planets in their place relation to the earth. Start with the one nearest the earth. (Mars, Jupiter, Saturn, Uranus, Neptune, Pluto.)

The four boxes of questions are placed on a table near the front of the room.

Draw two large baseball diamonds on the chalkboard.

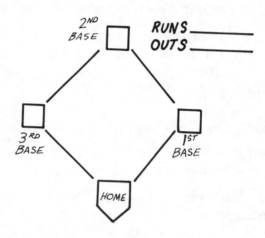

**C. Introduction to the Class:** I know we have some good baseball players in our class. How many of you like to play baseball? How many outs are there in an inning? What does the batter have to do to score a home run? Is it more difficult to make a home run than it is to get on first base? Who would like to tell us how the game is played? (This will probably involve several of the children in discussion.)

Today, we are going to play Space Baseball. We will play the game very much as real baseball is played except we shall make runs by answering questions about space. I have put questions in these four boxes marked — One-base Hit, Two-base Hit, Three-base Hit and Home Run. Which box do you think has the easiest questions? That's right, the one that says, One-base Hit. The most difficult questions are in the box marked, Home Run. You may choose the box from which your question will be taken. If you answer the question correctly, you will go to the base that the box indicates and the next team member is up to bat. Just as in baseball, you have to get around the bases to "Home" in order to score a run. If you miss your question, you make an out. Three outs and the other team will be up to bat. We will play three innings. At the end of that time, the team with the most runs wins the game.

Let's count off by twos. The "ones" will play on the left diamond and the "twos" will play on the right diamond. The "ones" will be up to bat first.

From what box do you want your question to be drawn? You want to try for a two-base hit? Draw out your question, read it aloud and let's see if you are safe on base. (If he answers correctly, place his name on second base and call the next child on the team.)

**D. Variation:** A diamond may be drawn on the floor of the classroom with chalk. The players will stand on the bases as the game is played. The teacher is the umpire and judges the correctness of the answers.

**E. Correlation:** This game can be used in any subject area for which the teacher can prepare questions; such as, social studies, arithmetic, weather, simple machines, etc.

## *6. I KNOW (Grades 4-8)

**A. Purpose:** To review and strengthen "space" vocabulary.

**B. Materials:** A sheet of 9 × 12 inch manila paper for each child. Scraps of colored paper cut into squares. A list of words from the vocabulary used in studying about space, placed on the chalkboard.

**C. Introduction to the Class:** Today we are going to play a game called I Know. (Pass out the manila paper.) Take this sheet of paper and fold it in the middle and then fold it in the middle again. Keep the corners right together. Now fold this up then over again. (Fold a paper while telling the children how to fold it so that they can see what to do.) Now open it up. You should have 16 boxes. Count them. Do you all have the right number?

I have a list of words on the board that we have used during our space work (about 40). Choose a word for each box and print it large enough to see easily. Do not copy them as they are on the board. Jump around when you choose the words. This game is more fun when each card is different.

(Give each child about 25 colored squares of paper.) I am going to ask one of you to play that you are the teacher and come to the board, point to a word, draw a line under the word and tell the class what the word is. If that word is on your paper, you are to place a colored square over it. When you have a row of colored squares going across, down, or from corner to corner, call out, "I Know." You will then pronounce to the "teacher" the words that you have covered.

—40—

*This activity is available in Inquire Volume I of the Spice™ Duplicating Masters.

If you cannot pronounce them, you have not won and the game will continue. If you can pronounce them correctly, you have won the game and we shall start a new game. I shall choose a new "teacher" for each game.

**Example of a word list:**

| | | |
|---|---|---|
| meteor | Jupiter | lift |
| galaxy | blast | eclipse |
| Little Dipper | air | Big Bear |
| North Star | weightless | Saturn |
| atomic | gravity | constellation |
| booster | satellite | astronaut |
| astronomy | solar | countdown |
| astrology | telescope | Mercury |
| Earth | drag | rocket |
| Milky Way | thrust | jet |
| Moon | rudder | orbit |
| Pluto | propeller | airplane |

**D. Variation:** Cards with words printed in the squares might be given to children. The whole card might have to be covered in order to be the big winner for the day.

**E. Correlation:** This game might be used in connection with simple machines, weather, earth science, animal and plant life, social studies, and reading vocabulary. Addition or subtraction facts might be placed in the boxes. The multiplication tables can be reviewed in this manner.

## *7. NAME THE CONSTELLATION
(Grades 4-8)

**A. Purpose:** To review identification of constellations.

—41—

*This activity is available in Inquire Volume I of the Spice™ Duplicating Masters.

**B. Materials:** 9 × 12 inch flashcards showing the different constellations studied; such as,
Orion, Cassiopeia, Leo, Scorpio, Ursa Minor,
Boötes, etc. These formations can be copied from
star charts found in many books. If they are not
in the books you have available, they can be
found in most dictionaries and in an encyclopedia.

FLASHCARD

URSA MINOR

**C. Introduction to the Class:** Let's divide
into teams and play a game about the stars.
(Divide the class into two groups.) One group
will be Team I and the other group will be Team
II. I will stand in the middle between the two
teams so that both teams can see me; but when
I am showing a card to one team, I shall have
my back to the other team so they cannot see
the card. (If there is an unequal number of
children, one child may keep score.)

I have made large flashcards that show the
stars in their constellations. I shall show a card
to Team I. If the right constellation is named,
the team will receive one point; then I shall
show a card to Team II and they will have a
chance to make one point. The team with the
highest score at the end of the game will be the
winner.

**D. Variation:** Older children may make the flashcards. This game may be used by individual children much as number combination cards are used. The cards may be used in the manner in which a spelling match is played.

**E. Correlation:** This game may be adapted for use in the study of simple machines, earth formations, animal and plant identification.

## 8. JETS (Grades 5-8)

**A. Purpose:** To learn what makes a jet plane move quickly; to prove that force in one direction is equaled in the opposite direction.

**B. Materials:** For each group: a balloon (long, not round), a drinking straw, nylon thread and adhesive tape.

**C. Introduction to the Class:** I know that some of you are very interested in jets. We have watched jet streams and have heard jets many times while studying about airplanes and space. When the airplane was first invented, everyone thought that we should never want to go any faster. Because there were so many places to go and so little time to spend getting there, inventors kept making airplanes go faster and faster. They finally decided that they could not make the propeller go any faster because it would not push the air back fast enough to make more speed. Air piled up around the propeller blades and speed could not be increased. They decided to get rid of the propeller and that is why the jet does not have one.

Since many of you are so interested, I think you might like to find out why a jet will go so fast. You can make a little machine that works in the same way as a jet works.

Let's get in our regular science-working groups and each group can perform its own experiment. You will find the materials needed on the work table. Each group may now get all of your materials. You need a balloon, nylon thread, a straw and adhesive tape. Place two of your chairs about 12 feet apart with the backs toward each other. Complete each step of the experiment as I tell you what to do.

First, run the thread through the straw and tie an end of the thread to each of the chairs. (The teacher will check to see that each group completes each step correctly before going on to the next step.)

Measure off four inches of adhesive tape and place it on the top of the straw, right in the middle. You will have about two inches of tape hanging down on each side of the straw.

Blow up your balloon. Keep the air from coming out by holding the end that you blow into. Fasten the balloons, at the middle, to the straw with the pieces of tape that you left hanging down. Do not let any of the air out of the balloon.

Now, all of you step back from your experiment except the one who is holding the balloon. Are you ready? Let go of the balloon. (The straw will move along the thread when the air rushes out of the balloon. The air moves out in one direction and the balloon moves in the opposite direction. Each group should repeat the experiment several times.)

Let's talk about what we have done and what we saw happen. (Allow for discussion time. Do not hurry the children.)

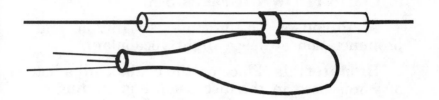

Newton proved that force in one direction is equaled in the opposite direction. Did we just prove the same thing? Did the force of the air rushing out of the end of the balloon make it move forward?

Now let's think about jets. Is there any connection between our experiment and the movement of a jet? (Let the children think this through orally. If needed, the teacher may use leading questions; such as, What makes the jet stream that we see? Lead toward the following conclusions but let the conclusions be developed by the children.

A jet works much as the balloon worked. A jet throws compressed gases backward just as the balloon threw air back. The backward thrust moved the balloon forward and it moves jets forward. As long as there is a stream of burnt gas coming out of the back of the jet, there is enough force to push it forward. This burnt gas is called a jet.)

**D. Correlation:** This experiment can be used when studying air pressure, weather and earth science. The experiment can be written up and placed in a booklet with other written experiments as a part of language arts work. The work of Sir Isaac Newton can be used for reading and book reports.

## 9. COUNTDOWN (Grades 5-8)

**A. Purpose:** To promote recognition and pronunciation of space flight vocabulary.

**B. Materials:** Place on the chalkboard a list of words used in the discussion and reading of space and space flights. Make 10 marks across the classroom with chalk. The tenth mark will be a box from which the "blast-off" is made.

**Example of vocabulary:**

| | | |
|---|---|---|
| gravity | lift | thrust |
| Atlas | docking | missile |
| satellite | capsule | atomic |
| Explorer | orbit | degree |
| Sputnik | Ranger | astronaut |
| explosive | Cosmos | spacecraft |
| rendezvous | hatch | three-stage |
| tracking | nose cone | Redstone |
| station | | |

**C. Introduction to the Class:** We have come in contact with some very exciting words while we have been working on space. I know some of them are quite difficult, but you like to use them, don't you?

We are going to pretend that we are astronauts in a rocket and ready for the last part of the countdown. We will start at 10 for the countdown. If we reach zero, our rocket will blast off. If we don't, then our rocket will be held because of poor weather conditions. We will have two big rockets and each rocket will hold half of the class. (Divide the class in half.) We will see which rocket will be able to blast off first.

Line up next to the first chalk mark. When

we get to the zero count, we will be in this box ready to blast-off.

I will point to a word in the list and the team which calls out the word first will start the countdown at 10. The next word will be countdown nine for that team. Each time a team gets the word correct first, that team will advance to the next line on the floor. When you reach the blast-off box, you may "take-off" and soar around the room. Are you ready to start the countdown? Who will blast off first?

**D. Variation:** Teams may take turns answering. One team may point to the words for the other team to recognize. This game may be played like a spell down and when a word is missed, that child must get out of the rocket.

**E. Correlation:** The name of the game may be changed and used with earth science, weather, electricity, and animal and plant life. Social studies and reading vocabulary may be used in this manner.

## 10. GRAVITY & DRAG vs. THRUST & LIFT (Grades 6-8)

**A. Purpose:** To review the concept of flight.

**B. Materials:** A list of questions pertaining to flight from balloon to rocket. Questions should be taken from work covered in class.

**Examples of questions:**

1. What was the first type of man-made flying apparatus? (Balloon.)
2. What type of fuel was first used in a balloon? (Hydrogen gas.)

3. What was the first machine to have a gasoline engine and propeller? (An airship or dirigible.)

4. Why did we quit using dirigibles? (They were too dangerous. They were easily destroyed by fire and storms.)

5. Who flew the first small flying machine? (Samuel Langley.)

6. Did people fly in Langley's machine? (No, it was too small.)

7. What holds an airplane up? (Air.)

8. Why are planes streamlined? (So there will be less drag.)

**C. Introduction to the Class:** Our game today is a contest between gravity and drag, and thrust and lift. We will divide into two teams. One team will be "Gravity & Drag," the forces that pull a plane down and the other team will be "Thrust & Lift," the forces that push a plane up. We will need one boy or girl who would like to play that he is an airplane making a flight. This airplane will stand in the middle of the room.

We have a list of questions about flight and flying. When a member of the "Thrust & Lift" team answers a question correctly, the airplane will go one step forward. If they miss a question, the plane will go one step backward. When the "Gravity & Drag" team answers correctly, the plane goes backward one step and if they miss, the plane goes forward one step. The "Thrust & Lift" team is trying to get the airplane on its way while the "Gravity & Drag" team is trying to ground it.

We shall see whether the airplane gets to make a successful flight, or if the gravity and drag is too much for it and it has to come down.

Are you ready for the questions? We will start with "Thrust & Lift" and see if we can get our plane started.

**D. Variation:** This activity may be used as a game with three children. It may be played on paper by moving a small airplane backward and forward as answers to the questions are given.

**E. Correlation:** This game may be used with the study of electricity to "turn the city lights on," or with work on sound to "break the sound barrier."

## 11. AIR FLIGHT (Grades 5-8)

**A. Purpose:** To promote understanding of air flights by man.

**B. Materials:** Three sets of questions about air flights by man, ranging from easy to difficult.

### Examples of easy questions:

1. What did men watch that made them want to fly? (Birds.)
2. Will a bird get out of breath when it flaps its wings? (No.)
3. Is air traffic decreasing or increasing? (Increasing.)
4. What does gravity do to a plane? (Pulls it down.)

### Examples of more difficult questions:

1. Why is the nose of a plane pointed and rounded? (So it can push through the air more easily.)

2. What is "blind flying"? (The pilot can see no landmarks.)

3. In what directions does a pilot steer an airplane? (Up and down, left and right.)

4. What is the new use for propellers? (As a brake.)

### Examples of the most difficult questions:

1. How does an airplane get a lift? (Speed and angle of climb.)

2. What causes drag? (Air rubbing against the plane causing friction.)

3. What does a pilot use to turn a plane? (A rudder in the back of the plane.)

4. What is the cruising speed of a jet? (About 600 miles an hour.)

Draw an airplane, a jet and a rocket on heavy cardboard and attach one group of questions to each. The common airplane will carry easy questions, the jet, the more difficult questions and the rocket will have the most difficult questions. Attach the drawings to a wire across the room or to a bulletin board.

**C. Introduction to the Class:** Today we are going to fly! We shall have four crews to man our ships and see which crew can take its craft the farthest. (Count off by fours to divide into crews.) Each crew select your captain.

Captains, we have three types of flying machines. Each type is carrying questions about air flights by man. The common airplane has the easiest questions and these are worth 10 points. The jet has more difficult questions and these are worth 20 points. The rocket carries the most difficult questions and these are worth 25 points. The captain will choose the type of aircraft for his crew. He will pull a question from the machine he chooses and the crew will answer it. If the crew answers correctly, they will score the number of points that it is worth. If they cannot answer it, they score nothing.

I shall keep score on the board. The crew with the highest score will have gone the greatest distance and will win the game.

**D. Variation:** Four children can play the game by themselves while the rest of the class works on other material. This game can be played without the aircraft and the questions can be put on the board but it is not as exciting for the children.

**E. Correlation:** This activity will work well with an energy unit using electricity, magnetism and friction. It will also be enjoyed during work with simple machines.

## 12. STREAMLINING (Grades 6-8)

**A. Purpose:** To show that air moving past a surface exerts less pressure than air standing still; to apply this concept to airplane flight.

**B. Materials:** For each group: four books, a tube from a roll of paper toweling, one piece of typing paper, a ping pong ball and a wad of paper.

**C. Introduction to the Class:** What is streamlining? Are sports cars streamlined? Are race cars streamlined? Why do you build your soap-box-derby cars low and narrow? Of course, it makes them go faster! Now, do you know why streamlining makes cars go faster? (This should result in a lengthy discussion since boys of this age are very interested in cars and soap-box-derby cars.)

A scientist named Bernoulli found that air moving past a surface exerts less pressure on that surface than air standing still. Our airplanes started out as box-like machines but now they are long and tapered. Do they go faster now than they did 30 years ago? Do jets go faster than the open cockpit planes used during World War I? Yes, they go many times faster.

Would you like to prove one reason why they go faster? It is because engineers have learned to use air pressure in a manner that allows for more speed. They have used the concept that Bernoulli proved. Let's see how it works! (Divide the class into working groups of four and provide the materials necessary for each group to experiment.)

Take the four books and put them on top of a desk, two in each stack about three inches apart. Put one piece of the typing paper on top of the books. Blow in the space between the books and under the paper.

Upon which side of the paper is the air moving? Does the paper move? On which side is the air still? In which direction did the paper move? Then, which exerts more pressure, still or moving air? (Discuss this thoroughly.)

Now, try blowing over the piece of paper. Hold it at the corners near your mouth. Does the end farthest away from your mouth move? What has happened? (Discuss this.)

Let's try something else. Take the paper towel tube and stuff one end of it full of wadded paper. Put the ping pong ball in the other end of the tube. Now, hold the tube by the end where the wad of paper is. Throw the ball out of the tube by a quick throwing motion. Slant the tube to the left. Did the ball curve? Which direction did it go?

Now try it again, but this time slant the tube to the right. Which way did the ball curve this time? Have we proved that air moving past a surface exerts less pressure on that surface than air standing still?

We will try a game using these tubes and balls when the weather is fair and you can see how this principle will work for you. (See the following activity.)

Now that we have experimented with air pressure, make a list of things that we have today that work on this principle. Let's make a contest of this and see who can think of the most things that work on this principle. We will count one point for each correct object and we will take away one point for each incorrect object. Is this a fair contest? We will have 15 minutes to work on this contest. Ready, start writing!

**D. Variation:** The experiment may be performed by one group at a time. This allows for closer teacher supervision but results in less child participation. Each child can perform the experiments by himself, using his own books and paper.

**E. Correlation:** All air and air pressure activities may be used with work on weather and earth science.

## 13. TUBE BALL (Grades 4-6)

**A. Purpose:** To use, in a manner enjoyable to children, the principle that air moving past a surface exerts less pressure on that surface than air standing still.

**B. Materials:** Two paper towel tubes, two wads of paper, two small sponge rubber balls that will fit into the ends of the toweling tubes.

**C. Introduction to the Class:** We have talked about air pressure and that moving air is wind. We have read and experimented to find out that air moving past a surface exerts less pressure than air hitting the flat surface of an object or air standing still. Let's go out on the playground and play a game that uses this principle. (Have the helpers bring the paper tubes, paper wads and balls. Go to the playground.)

We need two teams to play this game. (Divide the group and have each team line up, about 10 feet apart, one behind the other. The teams should face each other.)

The first player on each team takes a towel tube and stuffs one end of it full of paper. This is your bat but you do not hit the ball. You put this small ball in the other end of your bat. When I blow the whistle, each batter swings his tube and the ball will fly out. The batters must run to the other team, hand the tube to the first person in line and go to the back of that team before anyone else gets the ball and touches him out. Everyone on the teams may try to get the ball and put the batter out except the person who will bat next. He must stand still until the runner hands him the batting tube. The game ends when we have all had a chance to bat. There is no scoring so it is not a contest — just a game for fun. Are the two batters ready with the balls in the tubes? Notice how the ball flies when it leaves the tube. Ready? (Blow the whistle to start each batting round.)

**D. Variation:** The game may be played in the classroom using ping pong balls. In the room, in order to make less commotion, the last person in line on each team will be the only member who can get the ball to make the out. The game can be played without outs. Just bat, run, change batters and start again.

**E. Correlation:** Use this activity in earth science and weather to show the force of gravity, that flying objects tend to go straight and that wind is moving air.

## 14. FLY OFF (Grades 5-8)

**A. Purpose:** To show that a free-moving body tends to travel in a straight line.

**B. Materials:** A ball, jump rope and deck-tennis ring. (Other objects may be used if these are not available.)

**C. Introduction to the Class:** Did you ever wonder why rockets go straight up instead of going in a circle? Do you know why they do not curve in and out or do a loop-the-loop? (Allow time for discussion and imagine a rocket doing a loop-the-loop.)

Sir Isaac Newton proved that free moving bodies tend to travel in a straight line. Could that account for a rocket going straight up when it is started in that direction? Let's see if we can find out if this is really true. We will have to go out on the playground to try these experiments. I should like the helpers to bring a ball, one of the deck-tennis rings and a jump rope. (Go out-of-doors.)

One of you get on the merry-go-round and hold the ball until you are going around fast. One of you stand out by yourself away from the group so that the ball can be thrown to you. All of you remember that we are going to see if this ball will try to go straight even though it is being taken around in a circle. One of the helpers start the merry-go-round going and all of us watch the ball. (Change children and repeat the activity several times. Allowing for poor throwing, it can readily be seen that the ball is trying to go straight in spite of the circular movement of the merry-go-round.)

Now let's use the deck-tennis ring. Joe, will you take it and go away from the group? Turn 'round and 'round, then let the ring fly out of your hand while you are going around. The rest of us will watch what happens. (Let many different children try this to see if the same thing happens each time.)

We will try the same thing with the jump rope. It is a different shape and it might act differently when you let go of it. (Again, allow several to try the activity. Go back to the classroom.)

What did we do out-of-doors? What were we trying to prove? What did these different objects do when they "flew" out of our hands? Did they try to go in a straight line? We tried to make them go in a circle by going around. Did this make them curve or did they still try to go straight?

Do you believe that a free-moving object tends to go in a straight line?

**D. Variation:** Use a record player. On the turntable place small articles that the children have in their pockets. (Objects; such as, paper clips, whistle, pennies, stones or small toys.) Turn the record player on at different speeds and watch the objects fly off. Observe that the faster the turntable turns the sooner an object flies off; but always in a straight line. (Centrifugal force.)

**E. Correlation:** This experiment can be used in number work, measuring the distance of the "fly off" at different speeds and the variation from a straight line. The observations and conclusions can be written up for a language arts project, experimenting with use of the scientific writing methods. (See Teachers' Supplement page 190. This would be for the uppergrade use.)

# SECTION IV:
## "Weather"

# 1. HOT AIR, COLD AIR (Grades 4-8)

**A. Purpose:** To show the behavior of hot and cold water as they mix and relate this behavior to air masses.

**B. Materials:** 2 clear glass bottles which will stand one on top of the other, mouth to mouth, hot water, cold water, food coloring, a piece of white paper and a card a little bigger than the mouth of the bottle.

**C. Procedure:** Fill, level full, one bottle with hot water. Add food coloring. Fill the other bottle with cold water, ice cold is best. Add another color or leave this water clear. Place the card on the mouth of the hot water bottle. Be sure that the water is in contact with the card. Invert the hot water bottle on top of the other bottle. Keep your hand on the card so it does not slip. Carefully turn the two bottles on their sides so they are lying, mouth to mouth, on the table. Bottles with a flat side are best for this. If bottles are round, use blocks of modeling clay to prevent rolling. Remove the card and be sure that the mouths of the bottles are in contact so leaking does not occur. Place a piece of white paper behind the bottles so the class can see the interaction more clearly. (The hot water will move through the necks of the bottles, staying on top. The cold water will move on the bottom, since it is heavier. If the hot water bottle stands on top and the cold on the bottom, the mixing will take place slowly at the point of contact. If the bottles are placed cold on top and warm on the bottom and the card is removed, a rapid, tornado-like, mixing will occur as the hot water rises into the cold, forcing it down.)

**D. Introduction to the Class:** During weather reports, references are made to hot and cold air masses. When these masses of air meet, interaction takes place. The model we have here, using bottles of hot and cold water, represents this action. As I place the bottles on the side, watch to see what happens. Which is the hot and which is the cold? What will happen if we stand the bottles so the hot is on the bottom; so the hot is on the top? What can you conclude about the action of hot air and cold air?

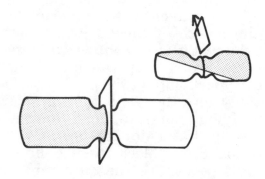

## 2. A RAIN GAUGE (Grades 4-8)

**A. Purpose:** To find out how to measure rainfall; to promote interest in observation of rain and its effects.

**B. Materials:** For each child: a ruler; a strip of paper; a small, straight jar; a pencil; a pointed paper cup; a quart milk carton; a jar about the same size across as the paper cup; adhesive tape and scissors. Have the children bring the jars and milk cartons from home.

**C. Introduction to the Class:** Grown-ups talk about the rain and how much it rained, when we have had a big rain. Have you ever heard them talking about how much it rained? Sometimes you hear that it rained an inch or two inches. Would you like to be able to measure exactly how much rainfall we have? If we can find out how much it rains here and you measure the rainfall at your house, we can see if the same amount falls on your house and on the schoolhouse.

Will you get the milk carton and the two jars that you brought from home? You will need your ruler and scissors. I have placed on the worktable a paper cup for each of you. There is water in this container and here is the tape when you need it. Listen carefully and follow the directions that I give you, step by step. If you need my help, hold up your hand.

(The teacher should read the following directions and be able to tell the children how to make the rain gauge without reading the directions to them.)

Cut the top off the milk carton and cut a large hole in one side of the carton. Pour water into the larger jar with the straight sides until you can measure an exact inch with the ruler. Put this water in the little jar. Cut a strip of white paper as high as the small jar and about half an inch wide. (The teacher should have these cut for the children.) Stand this paper beside the small jar and mark exactly where the top of the water is. Make another mark on the paper the same distance from the first mark as that mark is from the bottom of the paper strip. Divide the space between each mark into ten equal parts by measuring and marking with a pencil. Tape this paper strip to the outside of the little jar. Use tape and tape well so that the paper will not get wet. Empty the water that is inside the jar.

Cut the tip off the end of the paper cup. Put the small glass jar inside the milk carton. Place it so that the markings on the paper strip can be seen through the hole cut in the side of the carton. Put the paper cup in the top of the milk carton with the tip inside the small jar. This is the rain gauge. It should be put inside a larger container so that it will not be blown over and then put outside where the rain will fall into it. You will be able to tell the amount of rainfall by looking at the white strip. Each mark is one-tenth of an inch.

(The following illustration shows how the rain gauge will look when completed.)

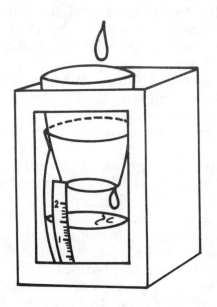

**D. Variation:** To make a very simple rain gauge, place a container, such as a coffee can, outside in the rain and when the rain has stopped, measure the amount by placing a ruler in the water. The part of the ruler that is wet, is the amount of inches it has rained. This can be used only in case of a big rain.

**E. Correlation:** The rain gauge project can be used in connection with earth science, plant life and simple machines. The marking and measuring may be used in connection with number work. A comparison of rain at home and rain at school may become a part of language arts through discussion and written reports.

## 3. GROWING WATER (Grades 4-5)

**A. Purpose:** To show that water expands when frozen.

**B. Materials:** For each working group: a jar with a lid, water, a paper bag large enough to contain the jar.

**C. Introduction to the Class:** Boys and girls, have you ever heard your parents speak of water pipes bursting when the weather is very cold? (Allow time for children to tell what they have heard.) Water pipes are filled with water. What happens to the water that makes the pipes burst?

The water grows or expands. When water freezes it takes up more space and there is not enough room in the pipes to hold the frozen water. Would you like to see what happens when water grows or expands? If you will divide into your working groups, I shall tell you what to do so that you will be able to see what happens when water freezes and expands.

Take one of the jars and fill it with water. Bring the water right up to the top of the jar. Put the lid of the jar on very tightly. Now, place the jar with the lid on it, inside the paper bag. Each group find a place outside on the window ledge and put your bag there. We will leave the bags outside overnight. (To do this, the temperature must be cold enough to freeze water. If it is not that cold, a refrigerator must be used.)

Tomorrow morning, we shall see what has happened to the water. Each group will get its bag and carry it very carefully to the work table. What do you think will happen when the water freezes and expands.

(**What will happen:** The water will freeze and expand so much that the jar cannot contain it. The jar will burst to allow room for the expansion of the water while freezing. The jar will be broken into many pieces.)

**D. Variation:** This experiment may be performed by one group while the others observe and discuss. The experiment may be performed at home and the children can then discuss what happened.

**E. Correlation:** When studying the environment of the earth, this experiment may be performed for the same purpose.

## 4. DO NOT BELIEVE ALL THAT YOU HEAR! (Grades 5-6)

**A. Purpose:** To prove that superstitions about weather are false.

**B. Materials:** A sheet of chart paper for each school month; gray, yellow and blue art paper.

**C. Introduction to the Class:** I know that you have wondered about some of the things that people say about the weather. There are many superstitions and sayings about the weather that you have heard and you did not know whether to believe them or not. What are some of the things that you have heard older people say?

I think you will enjoy finding out if these old sayings are true or not. There is a belief among some people that a crescent moon will hold water and the weather will be dry during that period. Others believe that a crescent moon will dump water and it will be quite wet during the time of the crescent moon.

In order to prove these sayings true or false, let's make a chart for recording the weather at the time of the month that the crescent moon appears. (Gray stands for snow, yellow stands for dry weather and blue stands for rain.) Keep this record for the rest of the school year. Draw your conclusions from the total picture observed on your chart.

**D. Correlation:** This activity could be used in social studies or in literature during the study of folklore.

## *5. MOUNTAIN CLIMBING (Grades 4-8)

**A. Purpose:** To review the seasons, how they affect man and the natural phenomena of weather conditions.

*This activity is available in Inquire Volume I of the Spice™ Duplicating Masters.

**B. Materials:** A mountain drawn on a large piece of cardboard with a steep path to the top. Imitation stones made from gray and brown paper with questions written on the front and the answers written on the back. Cut slits in the path and place each stone in a slit, with the questions outside.

**Examples of questions:**

1. Why do we use a barometer? (To show change of weather and see indications of fair or stormy weather.)

2. What is wind? (Moving air.)

3. What is fog? (A cloud near earth.)

4. What season is considered the time for removing storm windows? (Spring.)

5. What is the freezing temperature? (32°F.)

6. What is sleet? (Fine, driving ice particles.)

7. What is snow? (Crystals of frozen water formed directly from water vapor in the air when the temperature is lower than freezing.)

8. What is a cloud? (A visible mass of haze suspended at a height in the air. Water vapor gathered together.)

9. What does a thermometer measure? (Temperature.)

10. When may we expect to rake leaves? (Fall.)

11. What is a cyclone? (A strong wind blowing circularly, especially in a storm with violent winds.)

12. What is a hurricane? (A cyclone of large extent with a high wind force. Rain, thunder and lightning are present.)

13. What animals hibernate? (Frogs, bears, etc.)

14. How is a snowshoe rabbit protected in the winter? (The color and heaviness of its white coat of fur protect it.)

15. When does it rain? (When the molecules of water vapor become so close together that they bump.)

**C. Introduction to the Class:** We have a mountain to climb! It will be here for some time and you can climb it many times. You will find the questions will be different every few days, so climbing it again and again will be lots of fun. You must step from stone to stone until you reach the top. Read the question on the front of the stone. If you can answer it, you may try the next stone. If you do not know the answer, turn the stone over and you will find the answer on the back. You may not try the next stone until you are sure you have mastered the answer for the question on the first stone.

Have fun and race all the way to the top of the mountain! Try climbing the mountain when you have your work completed or when you are working on your science.

**D. Variation:** Use the questions on the stones to play a game between teams consisting of four children. The team reaching the top of the mountain first wins the game. When a question is missed, the team missing must wait until the next turn to try again. Two different paths may be put on the mountain so that each team will climb a different place and answer different questions. This will give eight children drill on two different sets of questions.

**E. Correlation:** Mountain climbing can be used in language arts, arithmetic and various science studies; such as, plant and animal life, minerals and rocks, uses of machines, etc.

## 6. MAKE IT FUNNY (Grades 4-6)

**A. Purpose:** Student appreciation of the Weather Bureau and its work; to show what might happen if we had no way of knowing what weather to expect.

**B. Materials:** Several cartoons from the paper, crayons or paints, drawing paper.

**C. Introduction to the Class:** Do you like to read the cartoons in the paper? Do you think they are funny? Do any of them teach us anything? Yes, some do. "Mark Trail" teaches us about wild animal life and "This Space Age" teaches us about rockets and planets. Cartoons can be funny, interesting and teach us a lesson, too. A cartoon has to tell us a little story of some kind. It may be only a picture, but there is a story for us to see. (Circulate several of the above cartoons around the class. Give the children time to look, read and enjoy.)

We have been learning about weather and how it affects our lives. We read or hear what the weather will be tomorrow, for a week and sometimes for the whole month. We often laugh when the weatherman makes a mistake, but he does help us to live better by knowing what to expect of the weather. People can prepare for hurricanes and bad weather of many kinds because they know about it in time to guard against ill effect.

Each of you gets a large sheet of newsprint and sketches an idea for a cartoon showing what might happen to you if you started someplace and did not have any idea whether it might be hot or cold, wet or dry, or very stormy. Imagine that the Weather Bureau has quit sending out the weather reports and we do not have any idea what to expect. Make this a funny picture, something that will make us laugh. The people and objects in cartoons can look funny, too. Sketch your idea on the newsprint, then get a piece of large drawing paper and draw your funny cartoon showing something that might happen if the Weather Bureau went on vacation.

**D. Variation:** A cartoon mural could be made by a group of children, telling the story in sequence.

**E. Correlation:** This activity will correlate with work on space, earth science, machines and animal life. A written story may accompany the cartoons and be used for language arts.

## 7. WATER THERMOMETER (Grades 4-8)

**A. Purpose:** To introduce the concept that materials expand when heated, contract when cooled.

**B. Materials:** Bottle, glass tubing or drinking straw, clay, a 3 x 5 inch card for scale, food coloring.

**C. Procedure:** Add some drops of food coloring to a clear glass bottle and fill it about 1/3 with water. With the clay, make a "stopper" for the top of the bottle. (Or use a cork or rubber stopper.) Make a hole in the stopper so that the tube or straw will pass through it. If using a glass tube, be certain to wet it before forcing it through the stopper. (The water lubricates the glass so it slides otherwise, the tubing breaks easily.) A length of one foot will be sufficient to show the rise of the water. To have the thermometer work well, the tube should be at least two feet long. Insert the stopper and tubing into the bottle so that the tube reaches to about 1 to 1½ inches from the bottom of the bottle. Plug the top of the tube with clay.

**D. Introduction to the Class:** Does anyone know how a thermometer works? (The enclosed fluid, mercury or alcohol, expands as it gets warmer because molecules of the substance move more rapidly and take up more space, even though no more molecules are added.) We can make one using water as the fluid. Do you think it would be a good one to use outside in winter? I have set up this thermometer using a bottle and tube, with colored water in the bottle. I am going to tape a piece of card to the bottle so we can mark the level of the water on it. I will mark the level where the water now stands in the tube. Now, watch the water in the tube when I put my hands around the lower part of the bottle. Why is the water level rising? (Heat from your hands warms the water.) What do you think will happen if we put ice on the bottle?

## 8. WHAT'S THE ANSWER? (Grades 4-6)

**A. Purpose:** To review and check knowledge of weather conditions, causes and results.

**B. Materials:** Questions made up by the children.

**C. Introduction to the Class:** We have been learning many things about the weather. I want to know what parts of our study you have enjoyed and what you think are the most interesting and important things we have learned.

Instead of asking you questions, I think you would rather make up questions to ask each other. Each of you will write out eight questions that you believe to be important. Of course, you will have to know the answers to your questions or you will not be able to tell whether your classmates can answer them correctly. It would be a good idea for you to write down the question and then put the answer under it.

Make up two true and false, two multiple choice, two completion and two why questions. We will use these questions to play a game tomorrow.

Let's work on the questions now. When you have two questions completed, let me look at them to see what you are asking.

**Tomorrow's Game:**

Place numbers on the board to indicate seating in the room so that each child will have a number.

**Example:**

| 5 | 5 | 5 | 5 |   |
|---|---|---|---|---|
| 4 | 4 | 4 | 4 |   |
| 3 | 3 | 3 | 3 | —seat numbers |
| 2 | 2 | 2 | 2 |   |
| 1 | 1 | 1 | 1 |   |
| 1 | 2 | 3 | 4 | —row numbers |

Each child will find the number of his own seat. This is his number in the game. Call on one student to start the review. He will state the type of question he will ask and then ask the question. He will go to the chalkboard and erase a number. The child sitting in that seat will answer the question. If he does so correctly, he may come to the board and ask the next question. If he does not answer correctly, the child at the chalkboard may call on a volunteer. If the volunteer answers correctly, he will be the next one at the board to ask a question. Continue until all children have had a chance to ask and answer a question. This will mean that all of the seat numbers will be erased.

**D. Variation:** The questions may be answered by children who volunteer. The rows may compete as a team, receiving one point for each correct answer.

**E. Correlation:** A review of this type may be used in any subject area to motivate the desire to review and to develop attention and alertness. It is especially useful in social studies, economics and science work on machines, space, the earth, animal life and plant life.

## 9. TAKE IT OR LEAVE IT? (Grades 4-6)

**A. Purpose:** To review facts about weather.

**B. Materials:** Questions written on strips of tagboard placed in a box ready for drawing. Children may make out the questions with the teacher's help.

**C. Introduction to the Class:** Today, we have a box full of questions ready for a contest.

We will pretend that this is the "Take It Or Leave It" show and each of you will be a contestant. We will divide into two groups by counting off by twos. The number ones will line up on one side of the room and the number twos will line up on the opposite side. I shall draw a question about weather from the box. I shall give you a clue as to what the question is about; such as, "This question is about storms. Do you Take It Or Leave It?" The first contestant in group one will have the chance to answer the question. If he thinks he can answer, he says, "I will take it." If he does not think he can answer, he says, "Leave it." If the question is taken, I shall read the question and if it is answered correctly, team one will score two points. If it is answered incorrectly, team two has a chance to answer. If a contestant says, "Leave it," the other side may or may not choose to answer the question. The side having the highest score when everyone has had a chance to answer a question, is the winner.

**D. Variation:** The class may be divided into several small groups. When the question is read, the group calling. "Take it," first has a chance to answer. If answered incorrectly, two points will be deducted from the total score of that group. Each group will work together to give the correct answer.

**E. Correlation:** This contest can be played in any subject area for which questions can be formulated; such as, animals, plants, machines, space, energy, social studies and economics. Arithmetic examples may be used in place of questions.

## 10. TICK TACK KNOW (Grades 4-6)

**A. Purpose:** To review work about weather.

**B. Materials:** Two large Tick Tack Toe frames drawn on the chalkboard. Prepare a list of questions or have the children prepare questions in advance. Use colored chalk to mark the frames.

**C. Introduction to the Class:** We have a game to play today called Tick Tack Know. We play this game like Tick Tack Toe. I have two giant Tick Tack Toe frames drawn on the board. We shall divide into four teams. Two teams will work on one frame and two teams will work on the other. I shall ask team number one a question; if it is answered correctly, an X is placed on the frame. If team one cannot answer the question, team two will get a chance to answer it. If team two answers correctly, an O is put on the frame. There will be a team one and a team two working on each frame. I will go from one frame to the other asking questions so that we can all play the game together. The team who gets three X's or three O's in a straight line first, wins the game. (Teacher picks four captains and the captains will choose the children for teammates. Each team lines up in a row, one child behind the other and the questions are asked in the same manner as words are given in a spelling match. Each child will place his own mark. Each team will use a different color of chalk.)

**D. Variation:** One team may ask questions of the other teams. A child who volunteers may be called upon instead of taking the children as they line up. One frame may be used instead of two, but more children will be waiting instead of playing if only one is used.

When a question is answered correctly, the team may be given a choice of placing a mark or erasing a mark of the opposing team.

**E. Correlation:** Tick Tack Know can be used as a game in the field of simple machines, space, earth science, animals, plants, social studies, spelling and parts of speech. It can be used for arithmetic review by using story problems for which the answer may be obtained, or examples may be worked by the whole team or an individual.

## 11. WEATHER SAFETY (Grades 4-6)

**A. Purpose:** To promote safety habits and proper attitudes toward safety during bad weather; to show that bad weather makes special measures necessary to maintain safety; to be used as a cumulative project for the study of weather.

**B. Materials:** Children will decide upon their own media of expression. They may need paints, paper, crayons, paste, magazine pictures, cardboard and black ink; or they may think of some unusual medium and a way to use it; such as, clay, papier mâché, copper wire, etc. The teacher may help them obtain and use properly the materials with which they choose to work with.

**C. Introduction to the Class:** Many times while we have been finding out about different kinds of weather, we have seen how it affects us in our work and in all living areas. We know that the weather can make it unsafe to drive or be out in the open. We have talked about different things that we can do to help us be safe during bad weather. I believe that others will be interested and will benefit if we share what we have learned. We can make posters and place them in store windows, in the halls at school and other public places where many people will have the opportunity to read our weather safety messages. Do you think this will be a good idea? I shall help you find places to display your posters. First, you will have to decide what you want your poster to tell others and then decide on the materials you will need to show your message. Try to think of some way to make your posters catch peoples eyes so that they will want to stop and read the message you have to tell.

We will work in committees. I will appoint chairmen and each chairman will select two others to work with him.

(Allow the children to start discussing what they will do and what materials they will need.)

**D. Variation:** Posters may be made by each child. A safety measure may be given to each group to illustrate. The posters may be incorporated into a mural that tells a connected story.

**E. Correlation:** Posters may be made in various areas of study; such as, animal protection, plant care, safety with machines, safety when using electricity, etc. Posters tell a story and may be used to give any message that the class wants others to know. Posters may be worked on as an art project.

# SECTION V:
## "Earth Science"

# 1. DISCOVERING LIMESTONE
(Grades 4-6)

**A. Purpose:** To discover limestone content of rocks.

**B. Materials:** Two bottles of Coca Cola, a piece of limestone, rocks from the playground, a box to hold the rocks.

**C. Introduction to the Class:** I have two bottles of Coca Cola. What do you think we are going to do with them? No, we are not going to drink them; we are going to test rocks to see if they contain limestone. Pour a few drops on this piece of limestone. Did you see the Coca Cola bubble up? Of course we knew that this was limestone, but we do not know whether the rocks we pick up from the playground have limestone or not. If the Coca Cola just runs off the stone without bubbles, we will know that there is no limestone content in the rock.

(The carbonic acid in the coke reacts with the limestone and releases carbon dioxide as part of the chemical reaction.)

We will have two testing groups. First we will go out on the playground and pick up stones. Bring all the stones that you find back to the swings and we will test them for limestone. All the stones that we find with limestone in them will be put in this box. We will bring them back to the classroom to examine closely and then we will crush them to see what might be inside of them. (This activity should last about 20 minutes.)

**D. Variation:** Suggest that the children test for limestone on the rocks that they find at home and then bring them to class and share their findings with the other students.

**E. Correlation:** If the locality is rich in limestone, this activity will be helpful in the study of local history.

## * 2. TAKE THE RIGHT PATH (Grades 4-6)

**A. Purpose:** To review and identify by name the various types of rocks.

**B. Materials:** A duplicated sheet for each child consisting of a maze puzzle with a box labeled "Metamorphic Rocks" at the end of the correct path. Along the way print names of many rocks of different kinds. The correct path to the box will have only metamorphic rocks named.

**C. Introduction to the Class:** Today, we have a puzzle to solve. You are trying to get to the rock collection at the end of the maze. Mark the correct path to follow. Find the metamorphic rocks and you will have the right path.

**Examples of Metamorphic Rocks:** Marble, Mica, Quartzite, Slate, Phyllite, Schist, etc.

**D. Variation:** A maze may be made that uses sedimentary or igneous rocks.

**E. Correlation:** A maze puzzle is suitable for use in connection with foods and nutrition. It would have a path following the protein foods, vitamin C foods, etc. Simple machines can use the maze theme to find types of machines. Heat and electricity paths can be found by following a path marked with types of heat or good conductors.

*This activity is available in Inquire Volume I of the Spice™ Duplicating Masters.

# 3. AROUND THE WORLD (Grades 4-6)

**A. Purpose:** To review minerals and where they are obtained.

**B. Materials:** Mount a world map on the board. Place pictures of different minerals around the outside of the map. Number the pictures on the back. Place a corresponding number on the map locating the place from which the mineral is obtained.

**C. Introduction to the Class:** We have a pencil game today. On the board is a world map and pictures of minerals from all over the world. On a sheet of paper, put the numbers that you see on the map. After each number, write the name of the mineral that is found in that location.

**D. Variation:** The class may be divided into teams. Each member of a team will connect a picture of a mineral to the place from which it is obtained by tacking a strip of paper from the mineral to the location.

**E. Correlation:** The study of animals, birds and plants can use this type of activity. Different types of vegetation and foods can be located in this manner. Social studies can use this activity to locate types of work and climate.

# * 4. VOLCANO GAME (Grades 4-8)

**A. Purpose:** To review materials from which volcanoes are made.

**B. Materials:** A large drawing of a volcano and the earth under a volcano drawn by the teacher or the children. Labels for the different

*This activity is available in Inquire Volume I of the Spice™ Duplicating Masters.

types of matter, printed on paper strips so that the children can fasten them in the correct places on the drawing.

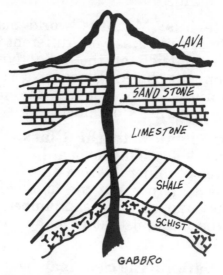

**C. Introduction to the Class:** Imagine that you are a bit of hot matter deep in the earth and you are seeking a way through the layers of the earth to the surface. Now, you cannot get to the earth's surface unless you can tell what each layer consists of. Later we will play the game by telling just what each layer is and, if it can be used, how we use it.

I shall point to a portion of our drawing and you will pick out the card with the correct label on it and place it where that matter is located on the drawing. (Point to a place on the chart.) Who wants to pick out the card with the name of the material that makes up this layer?

**D. Variation:** The children can fill in the names on a duplicated sheet containing the drawing. They may play the game by telling how we use each type of material.

**E. Correlation:** This activity can be used as a portion of the work on economics and social studies. The study of heat may include work on volcanoes.

## 5. VOLCANO ERUPTION (Grades 4-6)

**A. Purpose:** To allow the children to visualize volcanic eruption and to experience the emotional reaction to the noise and sight of an eruption. (Do not use this as a teaching process. Teach the concept of volcano formation first and use this as a follow-up.)

**B. Materials:** Old modeling clay, a small metal lid about an inch in diameter, two tablespoons of ammonium dichromate (buy from a druggist), a cookie sheet or a metal lid.

**C. Introduction to the Class:** We have talked about the power of volcanoes and how the cinders, ash and lava can build up into mountains. Would you like to see just how a mountain can be formed from matter deep in the earth? Would you like to see a volcano erupt? We can make a small ash volcano and imagine that it is big and real. We can imagine that the hot ash is coming from deep in the earth where a tremendous amount of pressure is forcing it to seek an outlet. We can see it and hear it erupt. How many would like to try this?

I have some old modeling clay from which we can shape the volcano cone. We will leave a small hole right in the top so that the hot ash can force its way out. (Give the clay to the children and let them start molding the volcano on a large cookie sheet.)

(CAUTION: The fumes produced by this experiment may be irritating. Do this outside or with adequate ventilation.)

After the children mold the volcano, insert a small metal lid in the hole at the top, about one-fourth inch below the surface of the mouth of the volcano. Fill the lid with ammonium dichromate. Hold a match to the ammonium dichromate until it ignites. The volcano will then spurt hot "ash" several inches into the air, and when it dies out and the children observe the enormous amount of "ash" covering an area two to four feet square, it is much easier for them to realize that mountains can be built little by little and layer by layer.

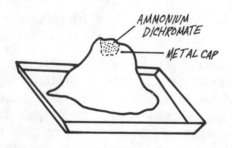

**D. Variation:** A cardboard volcano can be made on a Q-tip box. Cut a hole in the lid of the box. Fill the box with powder and put it back together. Run a small rubber tube into the end of the box. The children can blow into the tube with little puffs which force some of the powder out of the top of the volcano, resembling smoke. Each child can make one of these and have a volcano of his own. This will not show the building of mountains.

**E. Correlation:** The study of volcanoes can be used during work on heat and climatic conditions.

# 6. ANCIENT FORMS OF LIFE
(Grades 4-8)

**A. Purpose:** To display to others what has been learned about ancient forms of life; to review information on the four stages of life on earth.

**B. Materials:** A large cardboard carton for each working group. The top and one side should be cut out of the box. Sand, modeling clay, shells, colored paper, plastic wrap, wire, pictures of different forms of life or paper on which to draw them and grass.

**C. Introduction to the Class:** We have to use our imagination, as well as the material we read, to visualize life on earth in the past. Would you like to make a series of box shows for display so that others can see the life of the different ages? You will have to search for information on size, age and in what environment they lived.

We will need a group to work on the Age of Trilobites, the Age of Fishes, the Age of Monsters and the Age of Man. Who would like to work on the Age of Trilobites? (Select a working group from volunteers. Proceed in the same manner to select groups to work on the other three ages.)

When we have our box shows completed, we will invite the other classes and our parents to come and see our displays.

**Age of Trilobites:** This will be an underwater scene showing sand, long-stemmed crinoids, bryozoan and trilobites. The trilobites at this time were very large.

**Age of Fishes:** This scene will be partly underwater, but one portion of the box should show ground rising up and the lung fish, with legs partially formed, climbing out of the water. The water part can be enclosed in plastic wrap to make it look realistic.

**Age of Monsters:** This will be a dinosaur picture. Be sure that the dinosaurs are in proper proportion to each other as to size and perspective. Use pine trees, palm trees and giant ferns for background material. Probably the Brontosaurus, Allosaurus, Pterodactyl and Tyrannosaus Rex will be the most usable subjects. This is a land scene with just enough water for the Brontosaurus to stand in to help hold his body up.

**Age of Man:** This can be Early Man showing the mammoth and mastodon, with man living in caves. The environment surrounding these creatures is ice and snow with evergreen trees. Present-day man may be pictured living in a modern environment.

**D. Variation:** This same idea can be used to make four murals or three-dimensional pictures. All models will stand up against the background of the three-sided box.

**E. Correlation:** This idea is applicable to plant and animal life, imaginative forms of life on other planets and different stages of man's history.

## 7. GEOLOGIC TIME (Grades 4-8)

**A. Purpose:** To review eras of the earth and its inhabitants during each era.

**B. Materials:** A tree cut out of heavy paper fastened to the bulletin board with the eras printed in place.

(The illustration contains time units, eras, life ages and life forms which can be used for this game and many variations. Use only one topic at a time.)

**C. Introduction to the Class:** We are going to climb the tree of geologic time by naming one type of life which existed during a certain era. We will have a contest. I shall point to an era and you will write the name of a form of life of that time or you may draw a picture. When our tree climb is over, each of us will tell what we have written or drawn for each era.

**Example:**
Paleozoic — trilobite, armored fish, cephalopod, brachiopod, dragon fly.

Mesozoic — Brontosaurus, Triceratops, Tyrannosaurus Rex, Plesiosaur, Allosaurus, Ichthyosaurus, Pterodactyl.

Cenozoic — mammoth, saber-tooth tiger, eohippus, mastodon, man.

| | | |
|---|---|---|
| CENOZOIC 70 MILLION | AGE OF MAMMALS | |
| MESOZOIC 125 MILLION | AGE OF REPTILES | |
| PALEOZOIC 365 MILLION | AGE OF AMPHIBIANS | |
| | AGE OF FISHES | |
| | AGE OF TRILOBITES | |

**D. Variation:** The tree can be used to study rocks and minerals (1) by placing names of types of rocks or minerals on each branch and having the children pick out the stone or mineral of that type, or (2) by picking out a picture of it if the actual specimens are not available. **Example:** agate, basalt, quartz, flint, chalk, sandstone, hornblende, garnet, gypsum, limestone, shale and pudding stone.

**E. Correlation:** Geologic eras and time placements can be used during work on plants, animals, weather and the study of civilization.

## *8. LAND OR WATER (Grades 4-8)

**A. Purpose:** To review terms pertaining to types of land and water.

**B. Materials:** A list of terms such as:

**Land Terms:** crest, foothills, glen, peak, mountain range, pass, valley, slope, summit, ridge, plateau, plain, bed of stream, cape, delta, island, isthmus, point, peninsula, promontory, sand bar.

**Water Terms:** bay, brook, creek, channel, lagoon, mouth, pool, rapids, river, rill, rivulet, source, strait, spring, tributary, whirlpool, waterfall, lake, sea.

A drawing of a mountain with a river at the bottom and a camp across the river. This may be drawn on the board by the teacher or used as part of the work on land and water and drawn by the children as a wall mural.

**C. Introduction to the Class:** We are going to play a game about different types of land and water. I shall select a leader who will call

*This activity is available in Inquire Volume I of the **Spice**™ Duplicating Masters.

out a word from a list that I have put on the board. (The children may compile the list of terms.) We will have two teams who are trying to climb the mountain, cross the river and reach camp safely. The numbers that are on the drawing are the rest stops for the hikers. Every time a team member answers correctly, the team will proceed to the next rest stop.

When the leader calls a word, the first one of the team will call out, "Land" or "Water." If the leader said, "River," what would be the correct answer? "Water" would be right. Are you ready? One team stand on the right side of the room and the other team stand on the left and we will start our game. The team reaching camp first will be the winner.

**D. Variation:** This activity can be used as seatwork. Duplicated sheets containing the terms may be given to each child and he will write "land" or "water" after each term.

**E. Correlation:** Social studies and economics may find this game valuable. In science work, this game may be used with weather, plant or animal life. The list of terms may be changed and used in many areas; such as rocks and minerals, sound, heat and electricity.

## 9. AIR PRESSURE (Grades 4-8)

**A. Purpose:** To promote an understanding of air pressure and the damage it can cause.

**B. Materials:** A can, such as a ditto fluid can, a hot plate, a stopper to fit the can tightly if no cap is available.

**C. Introduction to the Class:** It is hard to believe that air can exert great pressure when we know that we breathe it, walk around in it and have it around us all of the time. We can see how much pressure air exerts by taking all the air out of a can and what power the air from the outside exerts when there is no air pressure to counteract it.

Plug in the heating plate, put a tablespoon of water in the can and put it on the heating plate. All of us will watch it closely and wait until the water in the can boils, then look for steam to appear at the opening of the can. When it steams we know that the air has been driven out of the can and that it is full of steam. Very carefully put the stopper in the can. Be certain that it is closed tightly. Carry the can to a cool place (or let cold water run over it). We will have to wait until the can cools a bit to see what air pressure will do to the can. While we are waiting, let's name ways we know of in which air pressure is used. (When the air pressure on the outside presses against the can, it will be crushed. It will completely collapse without anyone touching it.)

BEFORE          AFTER

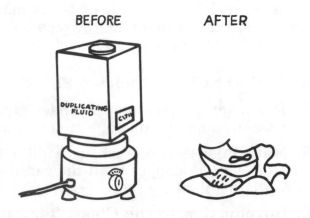

**D. Variation:** The following experiment can be used while waiting for the can to cool or it can be used alone to teach the same principle.

Each child in the class should have a glass and a cardboard square larger than the top of the glass. Fill each glass with water. Put the cardboard firmly in place and turn the glass upside down. Remove your hand and the cardboard will remain on the glass. Air pressure will keep the water inside the glass even though the glass is upside down.

The children should write up their experiments with air pressure telling what they did, what they discovered and of what use this knowledge is to us.

**E. Correlation:** Air pressure may be used during work on weather, heat, water and space. The work can be adapted for the study of fish.

# SECTION VI:
## "Light — Heat"

# Additional Teacher Information

**Heat:** a form of energy associated with molecular movement, i.e., the more heat energy in a substance, the faster its molecules will be moving. It flows from a high temperature region to a lower temperature region..

**Temperature:** a measure of heat energy or heat intensity present in a body of matter.

**Light:** radiant or luminous energy which travels in waves from a source at a rate of about 186,300 miles per second.

# LIGHT

## * 1. SHADOW LAND (Grades 4-6)

**A. Purpose:** To prove that shadows change at different times of the day; to determine how shadows change at specified times.

**B. Materials:** Notebooks for each student, a yardstick, small wooden stakes, a post or a long stick, a place out-of-doors in the sun.

**C. Introduction to the Class:** Have you ever noticed your shadow? What does it do? Sometimes it is in one place and sometimes it is in another place. Our shadow changes at different times of the day. Let's watch our shadows and see if we can tell how shadows change at different times of the day.

We can tell what part of the day it is just by looking at our shadows. The Indians thought that watching shadows was a good way to tell the time of day.

If we put a stick into the ground where the sun will shine and watch where the shadows are we can learn to tell what part of the day it is just by looking at the shadows. Let's go out into the sunshine and try an experiment with shadows. (Take along the materials.)

First, we must put this long stick in the ground. Watch the shadow. Now, place the small wooden stake in the ground where the shadow ends. Measure the distance between the stake and the stick. Write down the time and the length of the shadow in your notebooks. We will come back in an hour and see what has happened to the shadow. (At the end of the hour, take the whole group back to the shadow stick and place another stake at the end of the

*This activity is available in Inquire Volume I of the Spice™ Duplicating Masters.

shadow. Measure the distance between the end of the shadow and the first stick. Have the children write down the time and the distance that the shadow has lengthened. Do this at hourly intervals during this first day.)

We will form committees to check on the shadow for the rest of the week. Each committee must keep a very accurate record so that we can compare our results at the end of the week. One committee will check at 9 a.m., one at 12 noon, one at 1 p.m., and one at 3 p.m. Each time a committee checks the shadow of the shadow stick, they will write down the time and length of the shadow on the board so that the rest of the class will be able to have this information for comparison.

**D. Variation:** Groups may have their own shadow sticks in different places on the school ground and compare the difference of shadows at the same time of day. Shadows of trees or other permanent objects may be measured.

**E. Correlation:** Shadow time and distance may be used as a number project. The idea of telling time by shadows may take a group into research on a time-telling apparatus, such as the sundial. Science areas; such as, the study of weather, heat, the solar system and plant growth, may find this activity useful.

## 2. CAPTURING COLOR (Grades 4-5)

**A. Purpose:** To promote the understanding that light makes color.

**B. Materials:** A prism or a gallon glass jar of water, a large sheet of white paper or cardboard, crayons or paints, squares of colored paper.

**C. Introduction to the Class:** We have discovered that the sun is responsible for the colors we see. Today, we are going to capture that color and put it on paper. (Have the prism or jar of water placed where the sun will shine through it. Place the large paper in such a position that the colors will show. The entire class will be able to see the colors made by the sun's rays. To help students remember the order of the colors, suggest a name, such as ROY G. BIV.)

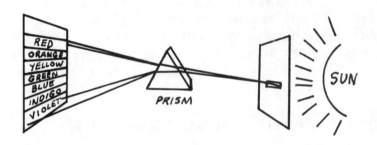

Find the crayons that you think will make the same colors the sun makes. Try them on paper to be sure. Who wants to place the first color on this sheet of paper? Can you capture the colors of the sun and put them on paper?

When the colors are captured on the sheet of paper, we will each make the same colors on drawing paper. These are the rainbow colors.

**(After the above work is completed: —)**

Let's play a game with our colors. Who wants to be "It"? "It" will hide his eyes while I put a colored square of paper on someone's back. "It" will try to see what the color is while the one with the colored square will try to keep his back away from him so that he cannot see the color. As soon as "It" sees the color, he will name it and the game is over. (Change children for each game and play several times.)

**D. Variation:** A color wheel can be made by the class and experimentation can be performed by mixing water colors to show how colors blend. The game may be played with several children as "It" and several having the colored squares on their backs. This could be a team game with the "It" team trying to capture the color of the other team.

**E. Correlation:** The color charts can be used for art in finding out what colors blend well together. Colors can be used to indicate heat of stars during work on space. This activity may be used in work on weather, heat and plant life.

## 3. LIGHT WILL BEND (Grades 4-8)

**A. Purpose:** To show that light rays bend when they pass through water or glass, making objects seem out of line; that light rays passing through air alone do not bend; that water in a jar acts as a magnifying glass.

**B. Materials:** Clean paint jars and a sharpened pencil for each group.

**C. Introduction to the Class:** Did you know that light will bend? What makes things visible to us? (Light) Can we see objects without light? (No) Would you like to make light bend and make a pencil look as though it is broken?

It is almost like being a magician. You can be a magician with the help of light.

(Divide the class into groups of five or six children. Each group will appoint a chairman who will get the materials with which to work.)

Fill the jar to the top with water. Place the pencil, point down, in the jar. Let the water become quiet. Look through the jar from the side. What do you see? Look through the jar from all sides. Look down into the jar from the top. Does your pencil look broken? Which part of the pencil seems to be larger? (Groups discuss what they have observed. Help them to understand that rays of light passing through the air, water and glass are bent and make that part of the pencil out of line. The rays that pass only through the air at the top of the pencil are not bent so that the pencil looks as it really is. The curve of the jar converts the jar of water into a magnifying glass and tends to make that part of the pencil that is in the water look larger.)

Find other things to try in the jar and see if they look broken. Each of you draw a picture showing what you have seen and then write a short explanation of your observation.

**D. Variation:** The experiment may be an individual activity with the children comparing results.

**E. Correlation:** The writing may be used as language arts. This experiment may be used during work on weather, space and plant life. (Using a small doll as an object to put in the water is very effective. The head will look as though it is floating on top of the water away from the body.)

## * 4. HELPFUL — HARMFUL (Grades 4-6)

**A. Purpose:** To show that light can be both useful and destructive.

**B. Materials:** A list of types of light compiled during work on light. Draw 12 chalk lines each a foot apart across a portion of the floor.

**C. Introduction to the Class:** We are going to play a game that will show us how light can help us and how it can be harmful. We will divide into two teams. One team will be "Helpful" and the other team will be "Harmful." Who wants to be captain of the Helpful team? (Select a child who volunteers as captain for each team and let each choose his team.)

Each team will line up behind the first chalk mark at the back of the room. The captains of each team will be standing on the line. I will point to a kind of light and the first member of the Harmful team will name one way in which that type of light might be harmful. Each time a correct answer is given, that team will move up one chalk mark. The game is won by the team reaching the last chalk line first. We will take

*This activity is available in Inquire Volume I of the **Spice**™ Duplicating Masters.

turns answering as we do in a spelling match. Are there any questions before we start? Line up with the captains standing on the first chalk line.

LIST              POSSIBLE ANSWERS

| | HELPFUL | HARMFUL |
|---|---|---|
| sun | makes plants grow | kills plants |
| fire | cooks our food | burns down houses |
| candles | decorate cakes | catch Christmas trees on fire |
| kerosene lamp | helps when the electric lights are off during a storm | smokes up the house |
| electric bulb | gives us light | hurts eyes if it is too bright |

**D. Variation:** This can be a seat game with such a list printed on a duplicated sheet. Each child will match the type of light with the "harmful" or "helpful" list. The one with the most correct answers will win the contest.

**E. Correlation:** Stories may be written for language arts telling how a particular light may be both helpful and harmful. A study of heat or electricity can use this activity in much the same manner.

## 5. LIGHT PROBLEMS (Grades 4-8)

**A. Purpose:** To promote realization of the speed of light.

**B. Materials:** Paper, pencil and problems.

**C. Introduction to the Class:** Light travels very rapidly. It can travel around the earth seven times in one second. The speed of light is about 186,000 miles a second. It travels 93,000,000 miles to the earth without being used up. (Put the above facts on the board.) The sun can send light to the earth in approximately eight minutes. Traveling 93,000,000 miles in eight minutes is pretty fast.

We will need our pencils and paper to find out the answers to these "light" puzzles.

1. How many times can light travel around the earth in one minute? $(60 \times 7 = 420$ times)

2. How many seconds does it take the sun's light to reach the earth? $(93,000,000 \div 186,000 = 500$ seconds)

3. How many miles will light travel in a half minute? $(30 \times 186,000 = 5,580,000$ miles)

(Discuss how the answers were obtained. Have the children work them on the board.)

Now, turn your paper over and make up five problems about the speed of light. We will use these problems in a contest.

(The following day, use these problems as a contest by dividing the class into groups of five members each, each group working together on ten of the examples. The group that finishes first with all answers correct will win.)

**D. Variation:** The class may be divided into two teams with one member from each team competing by working the examples on the board. The team whose member first works the examples correctly will receive one light year. The team with the most light years at the end of the period will win.

**E. Correlation:** This is arithmetic and can be used as part of the regular number work. The same type of activity can be used in the study of the speed of sound.

# HEAT

## 1. HEAT WORDS (Grades 4-8)

**A. Purpose:** To enjoy drill on vocabulary needed for the study of heat.

**B. Materials:** A list of words collected from the texts and from knowledge of what the teacher hopes to cover during the study of heat.

### Example of word list:

| | | |
|---|---|---|
| energy | steam | exposure |
| source | thermostat | electric |
| fuels | exhaustion | evaporation |
| thermometer | ventilation | gauge |
| degree | precaution | expansion |

Give each word a number. Duplicate the numbers and place them in a box. (Make several of each number if there is not a word for each student.)

**C. Introduction to the Class:** In this box I have numbers that correspond to the words listed on the board. We will draw numbers and see if we can pronounce and tell the meaning of the word that bears your number. If you can do this, you may keep the number. When we finish our contest, we will count how many numbers each of you has. Who wants to start?

When the drill is over, give each child a sheet of paper and five of the words from the list. Each child will write the meaning of each word and explain how this word might be used in the study of heat.

**D. Variation:** The contest can be used as a team game. One child might pronounce the word and another child give the meaning.

**E. Correlation:** This vocabulary will probably correlate with the study of earth science and weather. The drill idea can be used in all areas of work.

## 2. COLOR AND HEAT (Grades 4-8)

**A. Purpose:** To demonstrate that a colored surface will absorb more heat from a source of light than a white surface.

**B. Materials:** Colored paper or cloth, ice cubes, a source of light (or sunlight).

**C. Procedure:** Use two ice cubes of equal size. Wrap one in colored covering and the other in a white covering. Place them an equal distance from a light source or on the windowsill in direct sunlight.

**D. Introduction to the Class:** To see if the color of a substance helps it take more heat from the sun, we will do an experiment with ice cubes. What color clothes do you usually wear in the summer? Yes, we often wear white when we want to feel cooler in the sun. In winter, we wear darker clothes. This experiment will help us to understand why. Each group will have two ice cubes (or do one experiment for the entire class to see). Wrap one ice cube tightly in white and the other in black (or other dark color). Place them on the windowsill in the bright sunlight (or under a lamp). We will check them every 15 minutes to see if one is melting faster than the other. What do you think will happen?

**E. Variation:** Use two juice cans, one painted black, the other white. Place a cup of water in each of them. Check the temperature of each and record it on the board. Place the cans in the sunlight or under a lamp. Periodically check the temperature of each.

If there are banks of snow outside, place a piece of white and a piece of black construction paper side by side in the full sunlight. As heat is absorbed, they will sink into the snow. Try other colors, too.

Have children go to a parking lot on a warm sunny day and feel the cars of different colors to see if some are hotter than others. (The darker cars will be hotter.)


## 3. HEATING SPEEDS UP MOLECULES (Grades 4-8)

**A. Purpose:** To demonstrate that heating an enclosed unit of air causes it to expand.

**B. Materials:** A soft drink bottle or flask, candle or hot plate, balloon.

**C. Procedure:** Attach the balloon to the top of the bottle so it is tightly in place. Heat the bottle, be careful so that it does not break.

**D. Introduction to the Class:** To do an experiment to show what happens to air when it is heated, we will use this bottle, balloon and the hot plate. Can anyone think of an experiment which we can do with these things which will show what happens to air when it is heated? (Discussion.) We will attach the balloon tightly to the bottle so that the air which is inside is trapped there. Now, I will carefully heat the bottle. What is happening? Yes, the balloon is starting to inflate. How can you explain that?

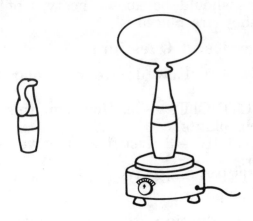

**E. Variation:** To illustrate that it is the air and not the balloon which reacts to the heating, when the balloon is well inflated, lift the edge of the balloon away from the bottle to let some of the air escape. As the bottle cools, the balloon will be forced into the bottle itself because outside air pressure is now greater than it is inside the bottle (since you let some of the greatly expanded mass of air from the bottle when you lifted the edge of the balloon).

## 4. A HOT CHART (Grades 4-6)

**A. Purpose:** To review concepts learned in the study of heat.

**B. Materials:** A chart showing a picture of different types of heat — the sun, electricity, wood, fire, gas, oil, battery, etc. Cut a slit in each object on the chart and place in it a card with a question and the place to find the answer. Change these questions often. The questions should be about the type of heat in which they are placed.

## Examples of Questions:

SUN — 1. How do we use solar heat in homes?

ELECTRICITY — 2. How can this type of heat help plants?

FUEL OIL — 3. List five ways we use oil as a helper.

BATTERY — 4. Describe a way that a battery helps in a car.

**C. Introduction to the Class:** On the bulletin board is a Hot Chart. When you have finished your regular work, you may take a card from the chart. You will find written on it a question and the place to look for the answer. These questions are about the type of heat that the picture shows. Take it to your seat, read it carefully and see if you can solve this "hot case."

When you have the answer completed, place the card with the question and your answer on the bulletin board for all of us to see. Be sure to put your name on it. See how many answer sheets you can have on the bulletin board during the week.

If you cannot solve the problem that you choose, the chart has "burnt" you and you must give the problem back to it. We will answer questions about these problems at the end of the week, so all of us will want to read them thoroughly.

**D. Variation:** The children can make up questions to be used. A simple list of questions may be used instead of a chart. The child would put his name after the question that he has answered.

**E. Correlation:** This activity may be used with any current science topic; such as, sound, light, space, earth science, weather and simple machines. The pictures on the chart should be changed to fit the topic being studied.

## 5. FOREST FIRES (Grades 4-6)

**A. Purpose:** To show that heat is destructive.

**B. Materials:** A box, newspaper, sand, detergent, soil, evergreen twigs and little rubber animals.

**C. Introduction to the Class:** Smokey the Bear is always warning us against fire and its destruction. We must have heat to live, but heat also can kill. Let's see what "Smokey" means when he tells us not to be responsible for starting a forest fire. Would you like to see what a fire in a forest can do without actually having a forest fire?

Take this large box and cut it so that it is about two or three inches high. Fill the box with sand. (If sand is not available, crumpled newspaper may be used.) Mix the detergent with water. Measure carefully. Use one cup of detergent to one-half cup of water. Cover the newspaper with this. Sprinkle a layer of soil over the sand or newspaper.

Use these little evergreen twigs to make a miniature forest. Push them down deep enough so they will not fall over. Now you have a forest and you need some animals to live in it. Put these little animals in different parts of your forest. (These should be rubber or some material that will not burn readily.)

Take one of your paint cloths and dampen it until it is wet but not wet enough to drip. Cover half of your box with this cloth. This is the part that we do not want to burn.

We will take our forest outdoors and set part of it on fire. (This must be done under very close supervision.)

(Follow this burning activity by making posters that will warn the public against the dangers of fire or too much heat.)

**D. Variation:** Two boxes may be used and there will be no danger of the fire spreading to the part that is not to burn. Other plants may be used instead of a forest. City children are more familiar with house fires. They could make two houses showing one destroyed by fire. It is not necessary to actually burn part of the exhibit in order to show the destruction. It can be built as the children would imagine it to look when destroyed by fire.

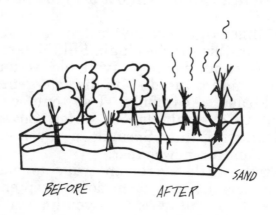

BEFORE          AFTER          SAND

**E. Correlation:** Use this activity during Fire Prevention Week when studying safety. It can be used during work on animal and plant life, the solar system and electricity.

# SECTION VII:
## "Sound"

# Additional Teacher Information

**Sound:** wave action in the air (usually). The waves of air move against the ear drum and are then transmitted to the brain for interpretation. The human ear can recognize sounds from 20 to 20,000 vibrations per second.

# 1. VIBRATION (Grades 4-6)

**A. Purpose:** To show that vibration causes sound.

**B. Materials:** Toy percussion instruments, two pan lids, three glasses of water filled to different levels, tuning fork, a large pan of water.

**C. Introduction to the Class:** What sounds did you hear on the way to school today? Did you hear any loud sounds? What is the most pleasant sound that you can remember hearing?

(Play a record of soft, sweet music. Allow the children to discuss the tone of the music. Play a selection of boisterous music and discuss the difference in sound. "Waltz of the Flowers" from the Nutcracker Suite, and "In the Halls of the Mountain King" are good selections.)

What is sound? Where does it come from? Can you imagine a world without sound? I want you to think about this and later we will write a story about an imaginary place where there is no sound at all. (Use for language arts.)

Now, let's see if we can find out what causes sound.

(Give percussion instruments to the children.) Strike your instrument. Do you hear sound? Feel the instrument. Is it moving? This movement of the instrument is called vibration. You can feel the instrument pulse like you can feel your heart beat. (Have the children feel their hearts.)

Strike your instrument and take hold of it. Did the sound stop? This is because we have stopped the vibration.

(Have one child strike the two pan lids together. Have other children observe the lids.)

Are the lids moving? Put your hands on the lids. Did the sound stop?

(Allow time for experimentation with the lids and the instruments.)

Put your hands on your throat and speak or sing. Do you feel movement? Was the movement in your throat something like the movement of the lids? (Bring out the fact that this movement is a vibration and that sound is caused by vibration.)

(Give a child the tuning fork and place a large pan of water on the floor where all can gather around to see what happens.)

Strike the tuning fork and we will listen to it. Touch it to make it stop. Did you feel it moving? It is vibrating.

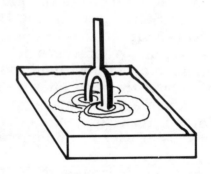

Now, strike the fork and put it in this pan of water. (Children will see waves move out from the fork.) The waves you see are caused by vibration. Strike it again and put the end of the prongs into the water quickly. (Water will spurt out and there will be a noise.) The vibration of the fork has so much force that it pushed the water out of the pan. (Let all of the children experiment with the fork.)

**D. Variation:** Other ways to test for vibrations are: Strumming on a stretched rubber band, playing the piano, striking small metal objects against water glasses containing various amounts of water and humming on a hair comb covered with paper.

This activity can be divided into several days work.

## 2. SOUND TRAVELS (Grades 4-8)

**A. Purpose:** To promote the understanding that sound travels.

**B. Materials:** For each group of two: a nail, two tin cans, several feet of wire or string and two large buttons. (These materials can be brought in by the children in advance.)

**C. Introduction to the Class:** Sound is sometimes carried over great distances. What are some of the ways in which sound is carried? (Telegraph, telephone, radio, television, echo, etc.)

Would you like to make a toy telephone that can carry your voice to someone who is some distance from you? Of course this is not the way a real telephone is made, but it will carry your voice so that you can talk to a friend. When you use this toy telephone, you will see that sound travels.

This is the way to make your telephone. Remove one end of each can with a can opener so that it is smooth and will not cut you. Punch a hole in the center of the other end of each can. You can use the nail to make the hole. Put the string or wire through this hole from the outside of the can and tie a button to it so that it will not slip out. Now, do the same thing with the other can and the other end of the string or wire. (Two children work together so that they have a telephone between them.)

Stand far enough apart so that the string is pulled tight. One of you speak into your can while one of you listens with the other. Do you hear the voice being carried? Now change and the one who talked will now listen.

(Children will be seeking the explanation of this. Help them to the conclusion that when a child talks into the can, the bottom vibrates. The vibration makes the voice much louder than it is when it has only air to pass through.)

**D. Variation:** The Morse code may be given to the children and they may tap out messages to each other with their pencils. The Morse code may be found in the Boy Scout Manual.

**E. Correlation:** This project may be used in language arts to teach telephone courtesy and communications. The activity may be used during the explanation of echoes in work on earth science. It may also be used while studying electricity.

## * 3. ANIMAL SOUNDS (Grades 4-6)

**A. Purpose:** To show that animals as well as people communicate by sounds.

**B. Materials:** A duplicated chart for each child, headed:

| ANIMAL | HOW IT MAKES A SOUND | HOW IT HEARS | WHY IT IS IMPORTANT THAT IT HEARS OR MAKES SOUNDS |
|---|---|---|---|

Under the heading of ANIMAL, list animals; such as, the giraffe, lynx, cricket, eagle, toad, etc. Have reference books and articles on animals, birds, insects and fish available for the children to use.

**C. Introduction to the Class:** Animals make sounds and hear sounds just as people do. They can communicate with each other. A crow will warn other crows of danger by calling in a particular way. A beaver will send his warning by slapping his tail against the water. I know people who think their pets communicate with them. Do your pets have a particular way of telling you things? (Allow children to tell of the sounds that their pets make. Dogs bark to indicate a stranger is coming. Cats purr when they are contented, etc.)

On this chart are listed many animals. Look up the animal and find out how it makes sounds. Find out how it hears. Write on the chart I have given you what you discover. Be sure to put the information under the correct heading.

—121—

*This activity is available in Inquire Volume I of the Spice™ Duplicating Masters.

**Example:**

| ANIMAL | HOW IT MAKES SOUNDS | HOW IT HEARS | WHY IT IS IMPORTANT THAT IT HEARS OR MAKES SOUNDS |
|---|---|---|---|
| giraffe | no sound | ears | Protection, cannot make sounds but it can hear and run fast. |

**D. Variation:** Sounds made by objects may be used. Children can listen to the sound made and write down what sound it makes, how it might affect people and how it is made, such as pencil tapping makes listeners nervous.

**E. Correlation:** This activity may be used during the study of animal life and simple machines. Language arts can make use of this type of activity.

## 4. SOUND IS A HELPER (Grades 4-6)

**A. Purpose:** To review how sounds help people.

**B. Materials:** A list of questions written on small cardboard discs that can be tossed into a box. Put the discs in a sack.

**C. Introduction to the Class:** Do you like to toss rings? Today, we have a game where we are going to toss discs into a box. You may not have a chance to toss one until you have answered a question about sound as a helper. In this sack, I have the questions written on the discs for you to throw into the box. Each of you will have a turn. Draw a disc, answer the question and see if you can toss your disc into the box. If you cannot answer the question correctly, you will have to give your disc to someone who volunteers to answer the question and he will get the chance to toss the disc.

**Possible questions:**

1. How can sound be used to cure people? (Ultrasonic vibration assists in cancer cure.)

2. What is cleaned by use of sound? (Buildings, clothings, etc.)

3. How does sound help in roasting? (A time clock may sound when the roast is done.)

4. How does sound help us in the morning? (An alarm awakens us.)

5. How does radio astronomy help? (Radio waves from stars help tell their size, distance, etc.)

6. How is sound used to tell if coal mines are safe? (Pipes are tapped on and the sound carries from one section of the mine to another.)

7. How does sound help us cross the street? (Car horns and automobile noise.)

8. How does sonar help us? (By plotting the depth of the ocean, finding schools of fish, submarines, etc.)

9. How does the Mach number help us? (It helps us count distance by using the speed of sound as a counting point.)

10. How does a fire alarm help us? (It indicates danger and will help us get to safety instead of being caught in a fire. It might call the fire department.)

**D. Variation:** Questions can be used as a test or as questions to be looked up and reported on the following day.

**E. Correlation:** The game can be used in any area of school work with appropriate questions put on the discs.

# 5. PROBLEMS IN SOUND (Grades 5-8)

**A. Purpose:** To promote understanding that sound travels at a fast rate of speed.

**B. Materials:** A list of problems dealing with the speed of sound. Information needed: Speed of sound in the air — 1,100 feet per second; in liquid or water — 4,800 feet per second; through solids, (steel) — 16,500 feet per second, (wood) — 11,000 feet per second, (aluminum) — 17,000 feet per second.

**C. Introduction to the Class:** Sounds travel rapidly but not nearly as fast as light. We see the flash of lightning before we hear the thunder. A navy man told me that they could see flashes of bombings long before they could hear the sound.

I have some interesting problems in sound for you to figure out. Read them carefully and see how many you can answer correctly. We will work them together later and see how much fun it is to understand the speed of sound.

### Possible problems:

1. How long would it take sound to travel from one end to the other of a piece of steel 10 miles long? (3.2 seconds.)
2. How long would it take sound to travel seven miles underwater? (7.7 seconds.)
3. How much faster does sound travel through aluminum than it travels through wood? (Six thousand feet per second.)
4. How many miles per second does sound travel through steel? (3.125 miles per second.)
5. If our voices were loud enough, how long would it take your voice to carry to a friend 500 miles away? (40 minutes.)

**D. Variation:** Figure the distance of a lightning flash by using the difference between the speed of light and sound. Use a time chart such as the following:

| Time between lightning and thunder | Distance of lightning flash |
|---|---|
| 5 seconds | 1 mile |
| 10 seconds | 2 miles |
| 15 seconds | 3 miles |
| 20 seconds | 4 miles |

The chart continues at 1 mile per 5 seconds.

**E. Correlation:** Problems may be used during the study of arithmetic, light, heat, electricity, earth science and weather.

## 6. CHIMES (Grades 4-8)

**A. Purpose:** To follow up the study of sound with an interesting building project.

**B. Materials:** Clay flower pots of various sizes; a pole, such as a long mop handle; a large rope, such as a jump rope; heavy wire, that is long enough to stretch across the room.

**C. Introduction to the Class:** We have been learning about sound and what causes sound. We have made sounds with many things. Do you want to make a musical instrument right here in class? I believe that we can make one and learn to play tunes on it.

How many of you think that you have some old flower pots at home that Mother does not need for a while? If you can find some, bring them to school. Bring one each of as many different sizes as you can find.

(It usually takes about a week to gather enough flower pots to actually make the chimes musical.)

Now that we have enough flower pots to make the sounds of an octave, we are all ready to start making our chimes.

(Tell the children how to make the chimes. Help them when necessary, but allow them to do the work of making the instrument and allow them to play it.)

**To Make the Chimes** — Use flower pots of graduated size. Hang the pots upside down with a cord large enough to be knotted so as not to slip through the hole in the bottom of the pot. Hang the pots by this cord from the long pole. Suspend the pole from a wire stretched across the room near the ceiling. Suspend the pole by tying rope to each end of it and then fastening the other end of the rope to the wire. The pots can be tapped with different objects to produce different kinds of music. Experiment with different sizes and arrangements until an eight-tone scale is formed. This scale should start at C to make playing tunes easier. Help the children pick out such tunes as "Good Night, Ladies," and "Mary Had a Little Lamb."

**D. Variation:** Drinking glasses filled with graduated amounts of water may be tuned and played with a spoon. Drinking straws may be cut at different lengths and blown through to make different tones.

**E. Correlation:** The chimes may be used in music and dramatic plays.

# SECTION VIII:
## "Electricity and Magnetism"

# Additional Teacher Information

## Electricity

**Static:** stationary electrical charges, i.e., not flowing as a current, but on the surface of objects.

**Current:** a flow of electrical charges.

**Magnetism:** a force which is the property of magnets, including the Earth itself, which attracts certain metals.

# ELECTRICITY

## * 1. A CHAIN REACTION (Grades 5-8)

**A. Purpose:** To promote the understanding of how a chain reaction works in connection with electricity.

**B. Materials:** A chain, dominoes, marbles, building bricks and a jump rope.

**C. Introduction to the Class:** We have heard and read the phrase, "chain reaction," in our science work. Electricity is caused by a chain reaction of electrons.

Just what is a chain reaction? A chain is made of many links held together. Would one or two chain links do us much good? When we pull on one end of the chain, what happens to the other end? (Let one child look up the word "reaction" in the dictionary and tell the others what a reaction is. Allow several children to pull on a chain while others observe.)

Divide the class into working groups. Give out the dominoes to one group, bricks to another, marbles to another, etc. Use any materials at hand.

The groups that have the dominoes and bricks stand them up in a row fairly close together. Those with the marbles, line them up about the width of your finger apart. One of you in each group lightly tap the end domino, brick, or marble. What happens at the other end? (Each hits the one next to it, causing the dominoes and bricks to fall down and the marbles to move forward.) Now change materials with another group and try the experiment again.

—131—

*This activity is available in Inquire Volume I of the Spice™ Duplicating Masters.

What did you observe? What did you find out? Each acts upon the object nearest it. Something started builds up and causes more action as long as something is near the object acting. Electrons bump each other like this.

Each of you is cautioned to walk carefully and keep your hands off others while going up and down stairs during a fire drill. Can someone explain why this is done? Is this an instance where a chain reaction could cause great danger?

**Follow-up:** Cause a chain reaction of your own. Observe what happens. Write up your observations. Draw a picture showing us exactly what happened. Use a sheet of paper folded into quarters. Label the quarters 1, 2, 3 and 4. Show us, step by step, what happened in the chain reaction. The last picture, Number 4, will show us the final result.

Observe what happens when you push the light switch, when Dad starts the car, when Mother makes toast, when you place a building block off center when building a tower. Find other things to observe. Bring your observations and explanations to class and share them with all of us.

**D. Variation:** Have a "tug-of-war." Let the children observe and feel what happens when one group overcomes the other or lets go of the rope. Discuss this after play time.

**E. Correlation:** The explanation of a chain reaction can be used in the study of earthquakes, volcanoes, lightning, heat, light and sound.

# * 2. CIRCUITS - OPENED AND CLOSED (Grades 4-6)

**A. Purpose:** To help students understand the term circuit and have them show the difference between an opened and closed circuit.

**B. Materials:** None.

**C. Introduction to the Class:** An electric circuit is a path over which an electrical current may flow with the aid of a generating device, such as a battery. When the circuit is closed, the electrical current flows through it completing the path and operating the electrical appliance. However, if the circuit is broken or open the electrical current is not flowing through the circuit and the path is not complete; therefore, the electrical appliance is not functioning. (Four ways of breaking an electrical current are: turning off the switch, removing a fuse, pulling the plug and cutting or disconnecting wires.)

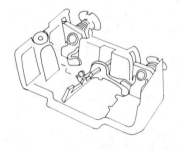 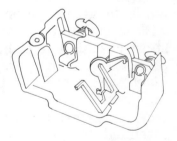

*This activity is available in Inquire Volume I of the **Spice**™ Duplicating Masters.

**D. Procedure:** We will make a list on the chalkboard of all the electrical appliances we can think of which need an electrical current to complete its path. After we have our list completed, we will go around the room and each person will take one word from the list and tell the rest of the class how we open and close the circuit to that appliance.

**E. Variation:** Have each individual, or groups, illustrate on art paper an electrical appliance showing the closed and open circuit.

## *3. SHORT CIRCUIT (Grades 4-6)

**A. Purpose:** To explain how and why we sometimes have a short circuit in our electrical wiring.

**B. Materials:** A diagram showing a short circuit, placed on the board and duplicated on a sheet for each child. Several boxes of cards numbered 0 to 20, extra cards containing the number "25," and many cards having only a red dot on them. Mix the numbers well.

**C. Introduction to the Class:** Electricity always tries to follow a straight path. It also tends to go the shortest way. When two wires without insulation touch each other, we have a short circuit. The electricity starts on its regular path through the wire and when it comes to the place where the two bare wires are touching, it jumps over to the other wire and returns to where it started without reaching the place it intended to go. If we have a short circuit, we push the light button but the light will not turn on.

I have a diagram drawn on the board so that you can see how electricity takes the short route.

Who would like to come to the board and play that he is the electrical current and show us what you do when you meet an uninsulated wire? (Let several children do this and then pass out the duplicated sheets containing the diagram.)

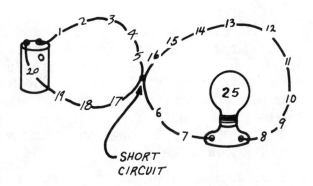

Now each of you has a diagram just like the one on the board. Make a red line showing how the electrical current would flow if it did not have a short circuit. Take your blue crayon and mark the path that the current would take if there were a short circuit. (Check to see that the children understand.)

We can play a little game using our short circuit sheets. Put numbers from 1 to 20 along your electrical wires. Put number "25" on the light bulb, "0" on the battery and a red dot where the two wires touch. The object of the game is to get to the light bulb and back to the battery, but every time you draw a red dot you will have to return to the battery and start over because you have a short circuit.

Cut a small piece of paper to use for the flowing electrons moving in your wires. (The children draw numbers from the number card box and move to the number that they draw. If they get past the short circuit to the light, they will start back to the battery. If they draw a red dot, they have to return to the battery. Divide into groups of five and play the game, taking turns drawing and moving. Have a box of numbers for each group.)

**D. Variation:** The children may draw their own short circuit diagram for the game. The class may be divided into two teams and the game may be played on the board. The teams will take turns drawing and moving. Chalk will be used to show where each team is.

Allow the children to play the game when their work is completed.

**E. Correlation:** This activity can be used during work on heat, light, weather and earth science.

## * 4. LET'S MAKE A MACHINE! (Grades 6-8)

**A. Purpose:** To use in an informative and practical manner the knowledge gained during the study of electricity.

**B. Materials:** For each group: a wide-mouthed jar, a cork to fit the mouth of the jar, aluminum foil, six inches of number 18 copper wire, a copy of directions and scissors.

**C. Introduction to the Class:** Would you like to have a machine that will tell you whether or not an object is charged with electricity? We know that electrons are moving all around us and are gathering on objects and then separating. Would you like to be able to find the

*This activity is available in Inquire Volume I of the Spice™ Duplicating Masters.

objects that have electrons gathered on them? We can make a machine that will tell us. This machine is called an electroscope and it will tell us if an object is charged with electricity. Here are the directions. (Write these out. Do not attempt to give them verbally. The children need to see what they are doing.)

**Directions:** Make a small triangle out of one end of the wire. Make a hole in the center of the cork. Run the other end of the wire through the bottom of the cork and bend the upper end in a spiral. This keeps the wire from falling back through the cork into the jar. The triangle of wire should be about halfway down in the jar when you put the cork in place. Cut the aluminum foil into a strip about two inches long. Fold it in the middle and hang it over the bottom of the wire triangle. Put the cork in the jar with the triangle and foil hanging from it. Now your machine is ready to test for charges of electricity.

(Rotate between groups and give assistance when necessary.)

Rub a comb through your hair until you think electrons have gathered on it. Touch the end of the comb to the wire spiral. If the two halves of foil move away from each other, the comb is charged. Now touch the spiral with your finger and you will see the two halves of the foil fall back together, showing that your finger is not charged with electricity.

This is the way the machine works. Now start testing materials for electrical charges.

(Have several electroscopes made by the class. Each group can test different materials and report to the rest of the class. See which group can have the longest list of materials tested.)

Keep the best electroscope in the classroom and encourage the children to keep testing materials and report on them during the school session.

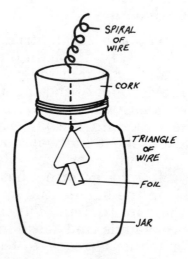

**D. Variation:** One child or one group of children may make the electroscope and explain what it does.

**E. Correlation:** This activity can be used with simple machines, heat and earth science.

## * 5. MAKING AN ELECTRICAL SWITCH (Grades 4-8)

**A. Purpose:** To make an electrical switch and show that it works on the same principle as the electrical light switch.

**B. Materials:** Three lengths of light insulated wire (one piece 11 inches long and two pieces 20 inches long), an 8 × 8 inch board

*This activity is available in Inquire Volume I of the **Spice**™ Duplicating Masters.

(2 inches thick), a 20 watt light bulb, a light socket (to fit the light bulb), #6 dry cell battery with terminals, wire cutters, 2 Popsicle sticks, hammer, 3 nails.

**C. Procedure:** Take 6 inches of the insulation off one end of both of the 20 inch long pieces of wire and 2 inches off the other two ends. Also take 2 inches of insulation off of both ends of the 11 inch piece of wire. Wind the 6 inches of uninsulated wire around one end of the Popsicle stick, one wire on each stick. Nail both ends of one stick firmly to the board. Nail only the wireless end of the other stick to the board (do not nail down firmly) so you can turn the Popsicle stick. Attach one end of the 11 inch wire to a light socket terminal and one end to a battery terminal. Attach the free end of the movable Popsicle stick to the other battery terminal. Then, attach the free end of the stationary Popsicle stick to the other light socket terminal. Insert the light bulb into the socket. Turn the movable Popsicle stick so the uninsulated wire touches the uninsulated wire of the stationary Popsicle stick completing the circuit and lighting the light bulb.

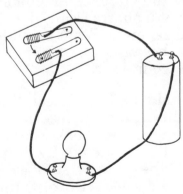

**D. Variation:** Divide the class into groups. Duplicate the directions for making a switch and have each group make an electrical switch as a project. The groups will know if they followed directions correctly if the light bulb lights up.

## 6. HOW DOES A FUSE WORK?
(Grades 4-8)

**A. Purpose:** To learn how a fuse works.

**B. Materials:** The switch used in activity 5 page 138, and a piece of thin tin foil.

**C. Introduction to the Class:** Today we are going to learn how a fuse works. Then, we will make one for ourselves. An electric fuse is a protective device for the electrical system. The fuse is a soft metal, with one point having a lower melting point, enclosed inside a fireproof container. When there is a problem in the electrical system, such as, a short circuit or too many appliances operating at the same time, the fuse will melt or blow breaking the circuit. This blown fuse indicates that something is wrong with the circuit and should be corrected. In the case of a short circuit, the short should be located and repaired. What should be done if the fuse blows because too many appliances are operating at one time?

**D. Procedure:** Disconnect the light socket and insert in its place a piece of thin tin foil. We now have our fuse. Let's see what happens when a fuse blows (melts). I will turn the switch to complete the path of the electrical circuit. What happened class? Correct, the thin tin foil gets warm and melts, breaking the electrical circuit. What happens when a fuse blows (melts) at home, school?

**E. Variation:** Bring in a good fuse and one that has blown (melted) show the class the actual fuse.

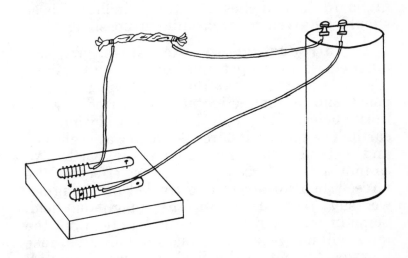

# MAGNETISM

## 1. MAGNETIC FIELD (Grades 5-8)

**A. Purpose:** To show the extent and effects of the magnetic field.

**B. Materials:** A bar magnet, a pencil, a pin, a nail, a piece of paper, iron filings, a piece of tagboard nine inches by twelve inches. These should be given to each child if possible.

**C. Introduction to the Class:** We use magnets to pick up things and to pull things. We have learned that the earth has magnetic poles and a magnetic pull is exerted toward these poles. This pull is exerted beyond the earth. The magnetic force is greater at each pole and extends out and around the earth. We cannot see this force but we see the effects of the force. When an object is attracted to a magnet, we say that it is in the magnetic field. Sometimes an object can be in the field but the force will not be strong enough to pull it because it is too far out in the field. The magnetic pull will be too weak to move it. Would you like to experiment with materials in a magnetic field?

(See that each child has the proper materials to perform each experiment.) Each of you place a paper on your desk. Put your pin on the paper and mark where you put it. Now, lay a magnet on the paper pointing toward the pin. Move it slowly toward the pin until you can see that the magnet has attracted the pin. Mark the place where the magnet first attracted the pin. Now put the nail where you placed the pin. You will find that the nail does not move even though the magnet is pointing toward it. The magnetic field went out this far because it attracted the pin, but it is not strong enough to attract the nail. The magnetic field extends for some distance but becomes weaker as it extends away from the magnet. This is the way the magnetic force of the earth reacts. The field extends far out into space but becomes weaker and weaker. Try this again and see if the results are the same. (Allow time for the children to experiment with different objects.)

Let's try another experiment with the magnetic field. Put the bar magnet on your desk. Place the piece of tagboard on top of the magnet. Sprinkle some iron filings over the tagboard. Tap the tagboard. You will find filings at the edge of the tagboard have not been affected by the magnet but those near the poles of the magnet have been affected.

Take the tagboard off the magnet and sprinkle the iron filings on the desk. Leave the magnet on your desk. Notice the pattern of attraction. This is the magnetic field where the effects of the force can be seen. The field extends beyond this but the force is too weak to make the filings move and the force effects cannot be seen. Move the magnet around and see the filings follow. Swirl the magnet. See the patterns that it makes? (Allow students to experiment with these materials until they can see the swirling patterns of force.)

**D. Variation:** The children may divide into working groups and experiment together. This will take fewer magnets and children do enjoy working together.

**E. Correlation:** The magnetic field may be studied during the work on earth and its environment and space. The patterns may be used as art work.

## 2. WE USE MAGNETS (Grades 4-6)

**A. Purpose:** To show that magnets are helpful and do work for us.

**B. Materials:** A collection of magnetic toys brought to school by the children. For each child a large sheet of paper, 3 square feet, with as large a circle as possible drawn on it. Divide the circle into eight equal parts as though cutting a pie into eight pieces.

**C. Introduction to the Class:** We have a fine collection of toys that need magnets to help them work. Will each of you who brought a toy show it to us and explain how it works? (Let each child have enough time to explain thoroughly and show the group just how it works.)

Now, let's talk about how magnets can help people work. (Children will tell ways in which they have seen magnets used and what the magnets were doing; such as, holding a tray on the dashboard of the car, holding a hot pad on the stove, picking up nails, finding parts that are lost in shops, removing something from the eye, etc.)

Give out the large sheets of paper to each child. Your paper has a large circle drawn on it and it is cut into eight equal parts. Draw a magnet in the center of the circle where all the lines meet. In each section of the circle, draw a picture depicting a way that we use magnets. Draw your pictures in the large part of each section near the outside of the circle. Below the picture in the smaller section, write how the magnet is being used. For instance, if you drew a picture of a stove with a magnetic pot holder, you would write below it that a magnet holds the hot pad so that it is convenient to use. If you have any questions, I will help you with them. When you have all eight sections completed, cut the circles out very carefully and we will display them in the hall for other classes to see.

**D. Variation:** A scrapbook of pictures of the toys brought in and the explanation of how a magnet is used in each toy may be made by the group and put on the reading table.

To show that a magnetic field is set up by a flow of electrical current, as demonstrated by the electromagnet, make a galvanometer. Make several wraps of insulated electrical wire around a magnetic compass, as shown in the illustration. Remove an inch of insulation from both ends and attach the bare ends of the wire to a flashlight battery by taping or holding. Notice the movement of the compass needle. Reverse the wires on the battery, by placing the top one on the bottom and vice versa. Does that make a difference? (The needle moves in the opposite direction. This device can be used to indicate whether or not a current is flowing in a wire.)

**E. Correlation:** The use of magnets may be incorporated in the study of simple machines and earth science.

## 3. WHAT IS AN ELECTROMAGNET? (Grades 4-8)

**A. Purpose:** To introduce the electromagnet and to show the class how one is made.

**B. Materials:** A nail, a dry cell, 2½ feet of light insulated wire, iron filings or tacks.

**C. Introduction to the Class:** Some jobs are too big for a magnet to do and electricity has to be used to give the magnet more power. This is called an electromagnet. It is used to pick up and load large or heavy quantities of some metals, such as iron and steel.

**D. Procedure:** Today, we are going to make an electromagnet. I will need a volunteer to be my assistant. (Choose a volunteer.) Paul, would you wrap this wire around the nail about 60 times. Then, I will remove about an inch of insulation from both ends of the wire and attach

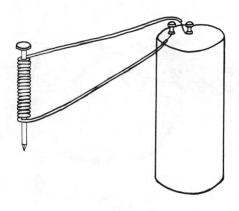

the bare wires around the terminals of the battery. Now Paul, hold the nail near these tacks. Did the nail attract the tacks? Now, disconnect one end of the wire from the battery. Hold the nail near these tacks again. Does the nail still attract the tacks? Why? (The magnet obtains its power from the electricity in the battery.)

**E. Variation:** Rewrap the nail about 120 times. Connect the wires again to the dry cell battery. Hold the nail near the tacks. Which electromagnet picked up the most tacks? Which electromagnet is stronger? Why does the amount of wire wrapped around the nail affect the power of an electromagnet? (Explain that an electromagnet is powerful because it is powered with a great amount of electrical current.)

# * 4. USING ELECTROMAGNETS
## (Grades 6-8)

**A. Purpose:** To make students aware of the common uses of electromagnets.

**B. Materials:** Use of the library.

**C. Introduction to the Class:** Who can give me some examples of items that depend upon electromagnets in order to operate? Yes, our telephones have an electromagnet in them and a doorbell also. (Students may guess such items as, tape recorders, motors, electric bells, loudspeakers, earphones, telegraph instruments, etc.)

**D. Procedure:** Divide the class into groups and have each group choose an item to research. They should then report to the rest of the class

*This activity is available in Inquire Volume I of the Spice™ Duplicating Masters.

where the electromagnet is located in their item and what its functions are. (A drawing of the item may be made for use by the groups for their presentations to the class.)

## 5. HOW DOES A TELEGRAPH WORK? (Grades 4-6)

**A. Purpose:** To show the students the basic principle of how the telegraph works.

**B. Materials:** The electromagnet made in activity 3 on page 146 (disconnect one of the wires from the battery terminal), and a thin strip of iron.

**C. Procedure:** Now, we will see how a telegraph works. I need a volunteer to assist me (select a student). Sue you hold this wire, you will be responsible for opening and closing the electrical circuit. I will hold this strip of iron close to the nail wrapped in wire. Sue, touch the wire to the dry cell terminal. What happened class? Let's try it again. Can anyone tell me what happened and why it happened? Yes, when the electrical circuit is closed the current is flowing through the circuit completing the path which magnetizes the nail. The strip of iron is then attracted to the nail. As the iron hits the nail it makes a click. These clicks which have been coded into dot and dash combinations form the Morse code which is used by telegraph operators.

## 6. LET'S MAKE A TELEGRAPH (Grades 4-8)

**A. Purpose:** To apply the principles we have learned about the telegraph into a project on making a telegraph.

**B. Materials:** Two blocks of wood, a dry cell battery with terminals, 2 lengths of insulated wire (one 12 inches long and one 36 inches long), 2 nails, 3 thumb tacks, 2 thin strips of iron each about 6 inches long and about 2 inches wide, a hammer.

**C. Procedure:** Take about one inch of insulation off of each end of the two lengths of wire. Nail the two nails (about one inch apart) into one end of one of the blocks of wood. Leaving about 12 inches free on both ends of the 36 inch wire, wrap the middle 12 inches around one nail starting at the bottom and working towards the top. Then, bring the wire over to the top of the second nail wrapping now from top to bottom. Insert the end of the wire leading from the second nail into one of the battery terminals. Using a thumb tack, nail one strip of iron into the end opposite the two nails forming the iron strip like the one shown in the following illustration. This piece is called the **sounder.** Now, nail one thumb tack into one end of the second block of wood. Nail the second strip of iron down with a thumb tack on the opposite end of the block of wood. This strip of iron is called the **key.** Attach the end of the wire coming from the first nail to the tack nailed to the key. Attach the 12 inch piece of wire (one end to the battery terminal and the other end to the thumb tack). The telegraph is now completed, therefore, we must learn how to operate it.

Can anyone tell me what the key is used for? Yes, the key is a switch which is used to close the circuit permitting the current to pass through with the aid of a generator, which in this case is a battery. Now, who knows what the sounder does? Correct, when the key is depressed the current passes through the completed circuit to the electromagnet which attracts the sounder. When the iron and nails meet, it forms a clicking noise. What happens when you let go of the key? Yes, the circuit is broken or open, therefore, the electric current cannot complete its path. Let each student try the telegraph, if he wishes.

**D. Variation:** Secure a list of the Morse code. Have each student write down on a piece of scrap paper the dot-dash combination for their first name. Then, let each student tap out his name on the telegraph.

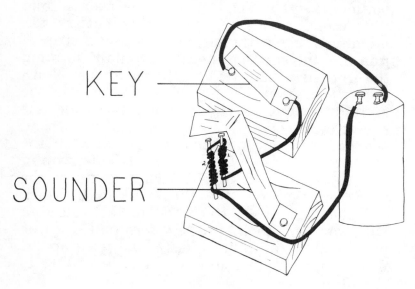

KEY

SOUNDER

# SECTION IX:
## "Plant Kingdom"

## Additional Teacher Information

**Plant:** a living thing, composed of cells, which usually contains chlorophyll which permits food production from light, $CO_2$ and water. Usually lacking mobility. (All living things, generally speaking, are either animals or plants.)

# 1. THE UPSIDE-DOWN POTATO
## (Grades 4-6)

**A. Purpose:** To motivate the study of plants; to promote the concept that plants grow from roots.

**B. Materials:** Two sweet potatoes, two identical jars, water.

**C. Introduction to the Class:** We know that plants grow from seeds and yesterday we read that some plants grow from roots. Do you believe that they do? Would you like to find out for yourselves by planting some roots? Good, I would too. What kind of roots would you like to try? Are there any foods we eat that are roots? Yes, carrots and sweet potatoes are roots.

This morning I saw some sweet potatoes in the grocery store and I thought you might want to plant them today. (Children like to bring things to school, so the planting could be planned for the next day.)

Fill these two jars with water and put the sweet potatoes in them. Leave the top of the sweet potatoes out of the water. (See that one of the potatoes is planted upside-down. If anyone notices that the potato is upside-down, say, "Which one is upside-down? Are you sure? I believe you are right, but let's leave it and see what happens.")

**Developments:** When one potato roots and the other does not, the children will try to find out why. Were they planted at the same time? Were they both watered regularly? Have they both been in the sunlight? Have they both had air? In this search for a reason, it may be discovered that one potato is upside-down.

Suggest that it be left and see what happens. "Do you think the roots will grow up and the leaves down?"

This potato will be slow to put out roots and even slower to put out leaves. When the leaves begin to grow from the bottom, talk about how heavy the potato is and how tender the leaves are. Will they be able to push the heavy potato up far enough so that they can grow up out of the jar into the fresh air? They will be able to.

**D. Variation:** Any root plant may be used. The children may each plant a sweet potato and the teacher will plant one upside-down. Let the children discover what is wrong with the teacher's plant.

**E. Correlation:** This activity may be used as a project during the study of health. It may become a social studies activity when the class is studying occupations, such as farming.

## 2. CARBON DIOXIDE (Grades 4-6)

**A. Purpose:** To find where carbon dioxide exists and to show that plants give off carbon dioxide.

**B. Materials:** A small bottle of limewater (purchased at the drug store), for each group; a drinking straw, a candle in a jar, a lid to cover the jar tightly.

**C. Introduction to the Class:** We know that we breathe in oxygen and breathe out carbon dioxide. We know that a fire will go out when it has no oxygen left. What are some of the other things that we have learned about oxygen and carbon dioxide? (Allow the children to discuss this thoroughly.) There is oxygen and carbon dioxide around us in many places. Would you like to make a test to find out where carbon dioxide is? (The children can make the test with the exception of lighting the candle.)

Divide into working groups and give the materials to each group. Put some of this clean limewater in an empty jar. Dip the end of the straw in the water and blow through it for about five minutes. You will take turns blowing. See the limewater turn milky? You have been putting carbon dioxide into the limewater and carbon dioxide always turns limewater a milky color.

Now, take the jar with the candle in it. (Be sure that the candle is short for safety purposes.) I shall light the candle for you. Cover the jar tightly and wait until the flame of the candle goes out. When the flame goes out, we know that the fire has no oxygen left to help it burn. When you are sure that the flame is out, drop a small amount of limewater into the jar and cover it again. What does the limewater do? Yes, it turns a milky color. What does this mean? That's right. You have found more carbon dioxide.

**D. Variation:** Put an open bottle of limewater and a plant in a jar with a tight cover. When it is dark, the plant will give off carbon dioxide.

**E. Correlation:** Use this activity during the study of the earth and its environment. When studying the lungs and the breathing process, carbon dioxide experiments may be used.

## 3. TREE AND LEAF IDENTIFICATION GAMES (Grades 4-8)

**A. Purpose:** To learn to identify trees and their leaves and to learn to spell and recognize their names.

### Leaf Domino

**B. Materials:** Prepare art board cards, four by two inches and place a drawing of a leaf on one half of the card and the name of a tree on the other half. The leaf and the tree will be different, as illustrated.

Make four cards of each kind to resemble dominoes. Put the cards in a box.

LEAF DOMINO

**C. Introduction to the Class:** We have a new game about leaves and trees that we can play like the game of dominoes. Each of you will draw three cards from the box. The first player places one of his cards in the center of the table. The next player must match the leaf picture or the name with one of his cards. The next one may play on either end, matching the name or the picture. We draw a card every time that we cannot play. The one who plays all of his cards first is the winner.

I shall put the game on this table and four of you may play at a time. (The children may make more games so that the whole class can participate at the same time. There should be no more than four children playing in each game.)

\* **Find the Trees of the Forest**

Place a box, such as this illustration, on the board or on duplicated sheets.

This work box is a clever forest and your task is to stroll around in it and name the trees you find there. The forester has planted more than twenty species of trees. He says the way to locate them is to start with any letter and spell out the tree names by moving in any direction, including diagonally, without skipping a square. You may repeat letters when desired. For example, find "C" and spell "Cherry."

(Clues to the trees: Cherry, alder, beech, elm, apple, ash, fir, maple, birch, cedar, yew, peach, mulberry, pepper, plum, fig, bass.)

| M | A | S | H | I |
|---|---|---|---|---|
| U | P | B | D | L |
| O | L | E | A | B |
| M | H | C | R | I |
| W | E | Y | F | G |

—157—

\*This activity is available in Inquire Volume I of the **Spice**™ Duplicating Masters.

**Tree Lotto**

**B. Materials:** Cards 9 x 12 inches, such as the one shown in the illustration. The leaves may be drawn or cut from magazines and glued into place. The children may prepare their own cards. Markers of colored squares of paper may be cut to cover the leaves.

This game is played just like you play Lotto or Bingo. The teacher may start off by calling out the name of a tree or some interesting fact about the tree, such as, "Cover the sugar maple," or "Cover the tree that has the name of a flower" (Tulip tree). To test how well they know the locations of trees in the community, call out, "Cover the tree that is in front of the post office," etc.

**Leaf Relay**

Have the children gather leaves from twelve trees. Use two or more teams of ten players each. Mix the leaves well in a box, then pour them out on the floor at the front of the classroom.

The teams line up single file and face the teacher. At a given signal, the first child on each team runs to the leaves and takes one leaf (any leaf) and runs back to his team, giving this leaf to the second player of the team. The second player takes the leaf and runs to the leaves and selects a different species of leaf from the one he already has, then runs back to his team. These leaves are handed to the third player who goes to the leaves and selects still a third leaf different from the two that he has. He goes back to his team and hands the three leaves to the fourth player. Continue in this manner. The tenth player will carry nine leaves of different species and select a tenth leaf, still a different species. The team wins which is first to select ten leaves of different species from the leaves. If desired, the winning team must also name each leaf correctly.

\* **Categories**
**B. Preparation:** Divide the board into three sections. At the top of each section write a major category; such as, food, decoration, building, etc. Below these, list six trees in each column. The children will need a pencil and paper.

**Example:**

| Food | Decoration | Building |
|------|------------|----------|
| maple | plum | magnolia |
| white oak | cottonwood | birch |
| ash | mulberry | dogwood |
| elm | banana | holly |
| gum | hackberry | palm |
| tulip | cinnamon | willow |

(Use the trees that have been studied in class.)

\*This activity is available in Inquire Volume I of the **Spice**™ Duplicating Masters.

Fold your paper into thirds to make three columns. I have written the names of some trees on the board. I have mixed them up under just any heading. I would like you to separate these names so that the names of trees that produce food will be written in the **Food** column, trees that are used for decorations will be placed in the **Decoration** column and trees that are used for lumber will be written in the **Building** column.

Put one of the words, **Food, Decoration** or **Building,** at the top of each column on your paper. Read the name of the first tree. Decide in which column this tree belongs and then write the name in that column. Go right on through the whole list of tree names.

### Gathering Leaves
The children may remain seated. The first child in the row starts the game by naming a tree leaf and each child adds one to the list. Each time a new leaf is added all the preceding leaves must be named.

Example: First child — oak; second child — oak, apple; third child — oak, apple, maple; fourth child -- oak, apple, maple, hickory. Whenever a child makes a mistake and calls out the wrong name or omits a name, the game is over and a new one is started.

**D. Variation:** Each game is a variation of the other and is used for the same purpose. These games may be used to identify plants; such as, flowers, weeds, vegetables, etc.

**E. Correlation:** These games may be used in work on earth science and animals by changing the words and pictures to fit the subject area.

# 4. MAKING MILKWEEDS USEFUL (Grades 4-6)

**A. Purpose:** To use materials collected during the study of plant seeds; to climax the study with an interesting, useful project.

**B. Materials:** Milkweed seed pods and seeds, cardboard sheets of various sizes, glue, tempera paints, small yellow beads, buttons (gold or silver), tiny Christmas tree balls, heavy yarn.

**C. Introduction to the Class:** We have brought a lot of milkweeds to school and so far we have used them only to look at, study and enjoy. We all thought it was fun to blow the seeds and see them fly through the air. We have many of them left plus quite a few of the old empty seed pods. Let's use a little imagination and see if we can think of something we can make from them that would be fun and worthwhile.

(Let the children use their own creativity as far as possible. There will always be some children who will fail to produce anything original. The following are suggestions that the teacher may give them.)

## Milkweed Doll

On the cardboard place half of a large empty seed pod, with the rounded part up and glue down tightly for the body. Use a smaller pod and glue each half into place for the legs. The arms will be made from a pod that is smaller than the leg pod, or if this is too hard to find, cut a pod into quarters and use a quarter for each arm. Draw the face above the body. Glue seeds with the floss still intact around the head of the doll for the hair. Use two seeds for each foot and one seed for each hand. Paint as desired.

### Christmas Poinsettia

Arrange the pod halves on a cardboard sheet in the shape of a poinsettia blossom, leaving a center an inch in diameter. Use half of a pod for each petal. Paint the pods bright red and glue into place. Run yarn down to form a stem with leaves. If green yarn is not available, soak the yarn in green paint and let dry before using. Glue the beads, balls or buttons in the center. Arrange two or three flowers in a cluster on a large cardboard sheet. Paint the cardboard before using if other than white backing is desired.

**D. Variation:** These activities are variations of each other. The closed milkweed pods may be painted and used as winter bouquets. Milkweed fairies may be made by gluing the seeds with the floss still attached to the cardboard sheet to cover the outline of a fairy's dress previously drawn.

**E. Correlation:** These milkweed activities may be used as art work. They may be given as Christmas gifts.

## 5. ADOPTING A TREE (Grades 4-8)

**A. Purpose:** To permit the class to study a single organism over an extended period of time and provide means to improve observation and note-taking.

**B. Materials:** A tree on the school grounds or in a safely reached area near the school, notebooks.

**C. Procedure:** Select a tree which can be studied for a period of a month or semester.

**D. Introduction to the Class:** How would you like to have a class mascot? Many classes and even football teams have mascots; such as, dogs, donkeys, birds, etc. How would you like to have a tree for a mascot this year? We can select a tree nearby which we can all study, sketch, photograph and watch for any changes which happen to it. We can learn its name, relatives, its value to man and other animals, what changes occur as the seasons change, what animals and other plants live in it and on it, etc. In the spring, we can watch the buds grow and open to show the new leaves which develop in the bud. (It is more interesting to choose a deciduous tree, one that loses its leaves, because more changes can be seen.)

**E. Correlation:** In math class, using triangulation, it is possible to determine the height of the tree, measure the circumference and the changing size of its shadow through the day or season.

As an art project, a bulletin board can be set up for weekly reports, photographs, etc., of the changing tree.

## 6. BABY PLANTS (Grades 4-6)

**A. Purpose:** To illustrate, by using actual seeds, that the seed contains the embryo plant.

**B. Materials:** Lima beans, popcorn seeds, etc., paper towel, transparent plastic cup.

**C. Procedure:** Have students soak the Lima beans (those from the supermarket will be fine) overnight in water. Wet a paper towel. Place the beans against the sides of the transparent plastic cup and "stuff" the cup with the wet toweling. Place in a dark area so the roots will not grow away from the light, but down the side of the cup. It is possible to wrap the cup in foil to make it light-proof. Open the seeds after a day. The form of the young plant will be developed. The bean will provide food for the growing plant until it is green and able to make its own food. (See the illustration of the Lima bean and the embryo.)

**D. Introduction to the Class:** Did you know that inside each seed is a baby plant? We can see this plant if we soak the seeds for a day or so because the plant starts to grow when it gets wet. Take the Lima beans (or other beans) and soak them for a few hours so they become soft. Then, we will place them in the plastic cup with wet paper to keep them from drying out. In a day or so, we will be able to open the bean seed up and find the shape of the baby plant. The bean will be the food for the growing plant until it gets bigger and turns green so it can make its own food.

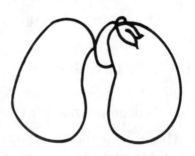

# SECTION X:
## "Animal Kingdom"

## Additional Teacher Information

**Animal:** A living thing, composed of cells, which is not capable of producing its own food as most plants are. It must rely on plants or other animals — which in turn rely on plants — for its food. Usually capable of mobility. (All living things, generally speaking, are either animals or plants.)

# 1. THE TREK (Grades 4-8)

**A. Purpose:** To review information about birds, fish, insects and mammals.

**B. Materials:** A chart drawn on a large piece of wrapping paper showing paths to be taken by the teams. Animals cut from magazines or coloring books, mounted on white paper with questions concerning insects, birds, fish and animals written on the backs. Prepare a master sheet of answers to be used by the children when they are playing without the teacher.

**Example of chart:**

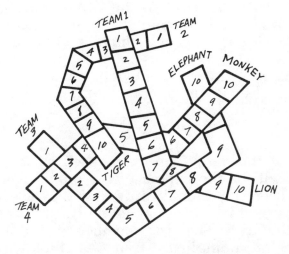

**Examples of questions and answers:**

**Insects:** 1. How do the antennae of the moth differ from those of the butterfly? (They are short and feathery while those of the butterfly are long and have knobs at the end.)

2. What are the names of the parts of an insect's body? (Head, abdomen, thorax.)

**Fish:** 1. What mammal do we speak of as a fish? (Whale.)

2. What fish do we have today that was in existence before the time of the dinosaurs? (Shark.)

**Birds:** 1. How do bird bones differ from those of a mammal? (They are hollow.)

2. What do we mean by migrate? (Traveling as a group from one place to another or one climate to another.)

**Animals:** 1. Name three animals that hibernate. (Bear, gopher, woodchuck.)

2. What is the life cycle of the frog? (Egg, tadpole, young frog, adult frog.)

**C. Introduction to the Class:** Let's go on a trek and see how many animals we can catch while on our journey. I have a game board on this sheet of wrapping paper. (Attach the chart to the bulletin board. Divide the class into four teams. Place the mounted animal pictures on the chalk ledge.)

We are going to travel over these paths and see which team can first reach its animal at the end of the path. The team reaching its animal first will be the winner of the game. The teams will keep the animal cards that they use and we will see which team has found the most animals on the trek. The first member of Team 1 will select an animal card from the chalk ledge and try to answer the question on the back of the picture. If the question is answered correctly, that team will move to Space 1 on the game path. Team 2 will have the next chance to select an animal. Each team will take their turns as they are now lined up. Each time a member of a team gives a correct answer, that team moves one space toward the animal at the end of the path. Are you ready to start the trek?

**D. Variation:** Ten questions may be put on the back of each animal picture. Each team selects one animal and the members will answer the questions on the back, taking turns with the other teams. Trek can be a game between individuals and played at the completion of other work. The sheet of answers would be held by a child not playing.

**E. Correlation:** Appropriate pictures and questions can be made so that this game may be used in many science areas; such as, simple machines, plants and earth science. Social studies questions may be substituted for science questions.

## 2. ANIMAL GAMES (Grades 4-8)

**A. Purpose:** To review material covered in animal study; to promote reasoning as well as recollection.

**B. Materials:** Pictures of animals cut from magazines, lists of animals and their characteristics, pencil and paper.

**Noah's Ark** (To review animal groups.)

**C. Introduction to the Class:** Today, we are going to help Noah put the animals into the ark. I am sure Noah would have wanted to put each animal in its proper group and we are going to play that we are helping him get these animals into their proper groups. Each of you select an animal and write down its name on a piece of scrap paper.

How many groups of animals do we know? Six is right. We will play that there are six floors to Noah's Ark. We will have a floor for each animal group. I shall draw six lines on the board to represent the six floors. Name the six groups. Write the name of a group on each of the lines as the children name them (insects, reptiles, birds, fish, amphibians, mammals).

Each of you will have a turn to come to the board and write on the correct floor of the ark the name of the animal that you have written on the scrap paper.

## D. Variations:

\* **1. Animals do not eat the same foods.**

Have the children list animals according to their eating habits; animals that eat plants, animals that eat animals, animals that eat both plants and animals. The children may find pictures of animals in magazines and place them on a chart instead of writing the animal's name.

\* **2. What Are We?**

For the younger children, place a list of animals on the board. Have them place the animal's names or draw their pictures under the proper heading — "ZOO," "WILD," "PETS," "FARM." This can be used as seatwork after the material has been covered in class.

**Example:**

| ZOO | WILD | PETS | FARM |
|-----|------|------|------|
| tiger | fox | cat | cow |
| lion | wolf | rabbit | horse |
| ape | raccoon | dog | sheep |

*This activity is available in Inquire Volume I of the **Spice**™ Duplicating Masters.

**3. Where Do I Live? (Matching Game)**

Place on the board a list of animals and a list of places where they live. Let the children come to the board and draw lines from the name of the animal to the place where we expect it to live.

**Example:**

| | |
|---|---|
| Bird | In the ground |
| Fox | Water |
| Fish | Jungle |
| Rabbit | Grass |
| Lion | Nest |
| Alligator | Den |
| Mole | |

If the lists are on duplicated sheets, this may be used as seatwork.

**4. Matching Parts**

The teacher places a list of animals on the blackboard. Ask the children to draw parts of these animals that are distinctive of the animal; such as, type of tail, feet, ears, etc.

This list may be made on duplicated sheets so the children can draw the animal parts as seatwork. If this is done, the children could list the parts on the board later and they should check their pictures to see if they are correct.

**5. Jumbles**

Names of animals may be jumbled and listed on the board for older children to unscramble. This may be done together or as individual seatwork.

**Example:**

| | | |
|---|---|---|
| shif—fish | rsoeh—horse | greit—tiger |
| peseh—sheep | inlo—lion | tca—cat |
| erba—bear | cwo—cow | barbti—rabbit |

**E. Correlation:** Each of these games may be used in the study of plants and machinery by making appropriate lists of plants, machines and characteristics. The teacher may enlist the aid of the pupils to make the lists.

## 3. OLD TRAPDOOR SPIDER (Grades 4-6)

**A. Purpose:** To acquaint children with a variety of insects.

**B. Materials:** Pieces of cardboard or tagboard cut 3 x 4 inches and pictures of different kinds of insects for the children to examine.

**C. Introduction to the Class:** We are going to learn many interesting things about insects. We will start by learning what the different insects look like so that we can identify them when we see them. We are going to make a card game by making insect cards. We will call this game Old Trapdoor Spider because he really is not an insect but only a close relative. While you draw the insects for the game, I shall draw the Trapdoor Spider on a card and this will be used as a "wild" card in our game.

I have pictures of insects in these books and you have pictures in your science books. Each of you will make four cards of the insect that you choose to draw. Who wants to make the picture of a grasshopper? Who wants to make the walking stick? (Continue through the insects common to your area.) Find pictures of your insect and make the pictures on your cards look as nearly like the real insect as you can.

(After the children have made the cards, allow them to play, five at a time, as part of their study period. After using the cards a few days, add some vital information about each insect on the cards.)

**The Game:** Play the game by dealing out six cards. The child to the dealer's left plays first. He will draw a card from the remaining pack and discard at each play. The object of the game is to get three cards of the same insect and lay them down. A wild card may be used with any two cards that are alike. The player getting rid of his cards first, is the winner.

**D. Variation:** The cards may be made large enough for the whole class to see from the front of the room. One card for each insect is all that is necessary. The class may be divided into two teams and the cards will be used as flashcards. The game will be played like a spelling match. A card will be shown to a team member who will identify it or be withdrawn from the game.

**E. Correlation:** Cards of this type may be made and used to acquaint children with plants, animals, fish, machines, rocks and minerals.

## * 4. WHAT'S MISSING? (Grades 4-8)

**A. Purpose:** To strengthen knowledge of the parts of an insect's body.

**B. Materials:** A simple blackboard drawing of an insect with parts of the body missing; such as, an insect with only two body parts, four

*This activity is available in Inquire Volume I of the Spice™ Duplicating Masters.

legs and one antenna. Drawing paper, pencil and crayons for each child.

**C. Introduction to the Class:** Look at my drawing. Does it look right to you? Yes, it looks a little odd. It is something like an insect, but it isn't an insect because it is incomplete. I have left part of it out of my drawing.

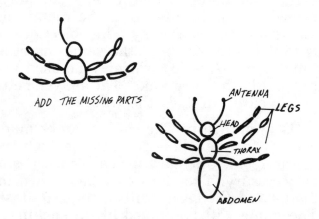

ADD THE MISSING PARTS

Take a piece of paper and draw my funny insect and then draw in the parts that I have left out. Make the insect large because I want you to label the parts of the insect after you have drawn it.

I shall check your work by giving you one point for each missing part that you draw in correctly and one point for each part that you label correctly.

**D. Variation:** The whole insect may be drawn on the board and some of the parts labeled incorrectly. The children would then get one point for each part that they correct.

**E. Correlation:** Parts of plants and parts of machines may be studied in this manner.

## 5. INSECT CAGES (Grades 4-6)

**A. Purpose:** To make a practical cage in which insects may be kept for study at home or in the classroom.

**B. Materials:** An oatmeal box, fine screen wire cut long enough to make a cylinder inside the box, six paper fasteners and a knife or pair of scissors.

**C. Introduction to the Class:** We have been bringing insects to school but we do not have a very satisfactory way to keep and observe them. I know many of you have been trying to study insects at home, but it is difficult to punch air holes that are small enough to keep the insects from escaping. Would you like to make an insect cage that you could use at home, or bring your insects to school for all of us to enjoy?

Each of you select a box, a piece of wire and six brass fasteners. Cut oblong windows in two sides of your box so that you may watch your insects. Make a cylinder out of the wire and fit it inside the box. Be sure to overlap the wire enough to fasten. Use the six brass fasteners to fasten the wire in place. Push the points of the fasteners through the box and the wire, then pull the prongs back tightly. Put the lid on your box. Now you have a fine, secure insect cage.

**D. Variation:** Use a pint glass fruit jar. Remove the center of the lid and replace with a piece of screen wire cut to fit.

**E. Correlation:** Small cages of this sort may be used to keep small animals, such as toads. Delicate plants may be put inside such a cage to avoid handling.

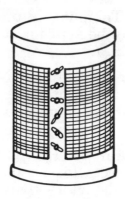

## 6. STATE BIRDS (Grades 5-8)

**A. Purpose:** To provide a learning experience beyond the structural study of birds; to acquaint students with birds of each state.

**B. Materials:** A road map of the United States for each group of four students. These maps may be obtained from gas stations. Cut 50 pieces of paper and print the name of a state on one side of each piece and the name of the state bird on the other side. Make a packet of these for each group of four. These can be found in any large unabridged dictionary or encyclopedia.

**C. Introduction to the Class:** We have something very interesting to do today. You know that each state has a state bird. What is our state bird? We are going to have a contest to see which group can put the state birds in the right state in the shortest length of time. I have made it easy for you because each group will have the name of a state on one side and the name of its bird on the other side. (Divide the class into groups of four.)

Here is a road map for each group. When I say, "Go," start through the pages of your packet, find the state and place the name of the state bird in the correct state. The first group to finish will win the contest.

**D. Variation:** State flowers may be used in the same manner. Pictures of the birds or flowers can be drawn or found in magazines and placed on a map to be used as a bulletin display.

**E. Correlation:** This activity may be used during the study of flowers, trees and animals.

## 7. BIRD GAMES (Grades 5-8)

**A. Purpose:** To review identification of birds.

### Ride a Rocket

**B. Materials:** A large half-moon and a rocket pointed toward the moon drawn on a chart. Small pictures of birds placed at different intervals around the outer edge of the moon.

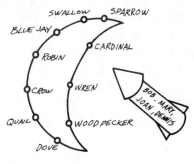

**C. Introduction to the Class:** Today, we are going to rocket to the moon. We have looked at bird pictures and named them many times. Now, we are going to play a game to see how many birds you can remember. I shall choose one of you to come to the board, take the pointer, point to the pictures and see if you can name them correctly. If they are all named correctly, you will get your name placed on the rocket. (Each child is given a chance to get his name on the rocket. If it takes more than one time for a child to be able to identify the birds, his name should be put on with a different color.)

\* **Birds in a Tree**

**B. Materials:** Shapes of birds cut from construction paper or birds cut from magazines; a large tree made from construction or wrapping paper and placed on the bulletin board.

**C. Introduction to the Class:** (Hold up a colored picture of a bird.) What is the name of this bird? Yes, it is a blue jay. What are the habits of a blue jay? Fine. Can anyone tell us something else about the blue jay? (Introduce three birds in this manner.) We are going to put birds in this big tree that I have on the bulletin board. Who would like to color these birds and put them in the tree? (Select volunteers.) We are going to put birds in our tree everyday for several days. You will all have turns to color one and put it there. When we have our tree filled with birds, we will play a game. We will have two teams and see which team can name the birds and tell the most facts about them.

—178—

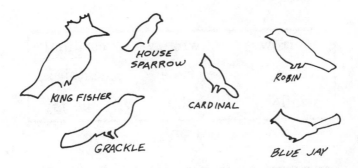

KING FISHER

HOUSE SPARROW

CARDINAL

ROBIN

GRACKLE

BLUE JAY

### Whoopee!

**B. Materials:** Prepare cards as for "Lotto" with nine squares. Write bird names on one side of the cards and words pertaining to birds on the other side. Prepare small cards the same way. The small cards will be read and used for checking. Make the cards different by writing the same words in different spaces. This makes two games, one on the front and one on the back. Make one side in black and one side in red so that the children can easily tell which side to use.

**C. Introduction to the Class:** I shall give each of you a card with bird names on it. I will read the same names from these small cards. When you see on your card a word that I pronounce, lay a marker on it. As soon as you have three words in a straight row either across or down, call out, "Whoopee!" I will check your card to see if you have marked the words that I have pronounced. If there has been a mistake, we will continue our game until someone does have three words in a straight row.

**Example of Cards:**

| sparrow | wren | cardinal |
|---------|--------|----------|
| crow | oriole | catbird |
| swallow | robin | blue jay |

(front)

| insects | beaks | wings |
|---------|-------|-------|
| toes | size | seeds |
| feet | nest | eggs |

(back)


**D. Variation:** Each game is a variation of the others. Each can be used as rainy day play. The last game may be played by three or four children after completion of their regular work.

**E. Correlation:** These games can be adapted for use with insects, animals, machinery and plants. The words used will be changed to fit the subject area.

# SECTION XI:
## "The Senses"

## Additional Teacher Information

Activities to use for developing and expanding use of the senses.

**Senses:** Seeing, hearing, touching, tasting, smelling — special nerve receptors which help us communicate more fully with the world around us.

# 1. SEEING SIDEWAYS (Grades 4-8)

**A. Purpose:** To make students aware of peripheral vision.

**B. Materials:** Two crayons or pieces of chalk.

**C. Procedure:** Choose a student to work with you in the experiment. Have him face the class. Stand behind him with a crayon in each hand, arms outstretched. Move your hands forward until he can see the crayons, while he gazes forward.

**D. Introduction to the Class:** I have an experiment in which we will discover how much you can see on each side of you. The volunteer will stand here and face the class. He will look at a spot on the wall so he does not move his head sideways. I will stand behind him, with a crayon in each hand. As I move my hands forward he can tell us when he can see the crayons, while he is still looking at the spot ahead.

**E. Variation:** Have students stand and name all the objects they can see beside them and in front of them in the room, while looking forward.

# * 2. TASTING (Grades 4-8)

**A. Purpose:** To introduce students to the four basic tastes; salty, sour, sweet, bitter.

**B. Materials:** Lemon juice, sugar water, aspirin water, salt water, paper cups, tooth picks, slices of potato, apple, onion.

*This activity is available in Inquire Volume I of the **Spice**™ Duplicating Masters.

**C. Introduction to the Class:** We often know how food will "taste" before we put it in our mouths. Why is that? (Discussion about smell and taste.) Why does food taste flat when we have a cold in the head? Yes, the odors or aromas are not sensed at that time. What tastes do we get then? Only the four basic tastes which are on the tongue. We will do an experiment to try to determine what part of the tongue has nerve endings to sense each of those four basic tastes. We have four solutions — salt water, sugar water, aspirin water, lemon juice. Work in small groups. Each group will need a cup of each solution and some toothpicks for placing drops of each solution on the tongue. Try to decide which part of the tongue, the tip, middle or edges, sense the taste of each most strongly. (On the tongue, sweet is sensed at the tip, bitter on the mid-top of the tongue, salt and sour along the edges.) Make a sketch of the tongue on your paper and mark the area where you get the best response for each taste.

There are also slices of onion, potato and apple. Hold your nose tightly and close your eyes when one of your teammates gives you a slice to taste. Can you identify it without the benefit of smell? Keep a record of your accuracy and we will put the results on the board.

**D. Procedure:** Students should place a drop of the test solution on several parts of the tongue and record where its taste is best noted. For tasting the slices, students may be blindfolded and close their eyes so they do not see the slice. It should be placed on the tongue for them by a teammate.

### 3. HEARING WITH ONE EAR (Grades 4-8)

**A. Purpose:** To emphasize the importance of using both ears to locate sounds.

**B. Materials:** Cotton for ear plugs, objects to drop, blindfold.

**C. Introduction to the Class:** Have you ever tried to locate sounds coming from some source that cannot be seen? How do you locate the direction from which the sounds come? By turning your head a bit from side to side as you listen? Why can this help? (It permits the hearer to decide from which side the sound is stronger.) Work in groups of three. One person will be blindfolded and have a cotton plug put in one ear. Then one of the other members will make sounds by dropping objects around him. Can he tell from which direction the sound comes? Let's try it.

**D. Correlation:** To emphasize the importance of having a pair of ears or eyes, correlate this activity with the Seeing With One Eye activity, which follows.

### 4. SEEING WITH ONE EYE (Grades 4-8)

**A. Purpose:** To demonstrate that one can see more accurately with two eyes than with one.

**B. Materials:** A patch of paper towel, masking tape, rubber ball (or paper wad).

**C. Procedure:** Have students cover one eye and try to play catch; then use both eyes.

**D. Introduction to the Class:** When we see, it is better to have two eyes so we can see more. We will choose two students to play catch. (Choose.) First, play catch with this ball, you are doing well. Do not throw hard. Now, let us tape a patch over one eye so each of you has only one eye. (Tape the patch of paper towel over one eye.) Try playing catch. Why did you miss the ball? (Discuss.)

# SECTION XII:
## "Teacher's Supplement"

# 1. PUZZLES (Grades 4-8)

## A. Puzzle Card

Is it hot or cold when the temperature is 20 degrees? _____

What kind of a machine is a see-saw? _____

When a fuse is blown, the lights go _____ .

Warm air goes _____ .

In what direction do roots grow? _____

The first letter of each word that answers a question can be put together to answer this question.

QUESTION: Fog is a low _____ .

## Answer Card

cold, lever, out, up, down

## Puzzle Card

A spring flower that grows in the woods. ____

A shellfish that we put in dressing._____

A simple machine that lifts. _____

What is the name for 2,000 pounds? _____

The first letters of the answer words spell a word used in electricity.

## Answer Card

violet, oyster, lever, ton

*   ## B. What Does It Spell?
    Use the letters of the alphabet to solve this puzzle.

| | | Animals That Live in Groups | Answers |
|---|---|---|---|
| A — | 1 | 19-8-5-5-16 | sheep |
| B — | 2 | 7-15-1-20-19 | goats |
| C — | 3 | 5-12-5-16-8-1-14-20-19 | elephants |
| D — | 4 | 3-15-23-19 | cows |
| E — | 5 | 2-5-1-22-5-18-19 | beavers |
| F — | 6 | 23-9-12-4   8-15-18-19-5-19 | wild horses |
| G — | 7 | 12-9-15-14-19 | lions |
| H — | 8 | | |
| I — | 9 | **Animals That Live Alone** | |
| J — | 10 | 20-9-7-5-18-19 | tigers |
| K — | 11 | 18-1-3-3-15-15-14-19 | raccoons |
| L — | 12 | 19-11-21-14-11-19 | skunks |
| M — | 13 | 19-17-21-9-18-18-5-12-19 | squirrels |
| N — | 14 | 2-5-1-18-19 | bears |
| O — | 15 | | |
| P — | 16 | **Animals That Lay Eggs** | |
| Q — | 17 | 20-21-18-20-12-5-19 | turtles |
| R — | 18 | 19-14-1-11-5-19 | snakes |
| S — | 19 | 12-9-26-1-18-4-19 | lizards |
| T — | 20 | 1-12-12-9-7-1-20-15-18-19 | alligators |
| U — | 21 | 2-9-18-4-19 | birds |
| V — | 22 | | |
| W — | 23 | | |
| X — | 24 | | |
| Y — | 25 | | |
| Z — | 26 | | |

* ## 2. PLANNING SCIENTIFIC EXPERIMENTS (Grades 4-8)

For children who are old enough to understand the concept of a "Control" factor in an experiment, investigations can be planned with the students. The so-called "scientific method" in actual practice in research laboratories is more myth than fact, but a general outline for planning scientific investigations is this:

*This activity is available in Inquire Volume I of the Spice™ Duplicating Masters.

a. Define the problem that you wish to investigate or the question you are asking.

b. Gather preliminary information from books, experts and your own experimenting to decide on a course of action for the investigation.

c. Formulate a hypothesis or a "guess" based on step #b concerning a probable solution to the problem. What looks like a reasonable solution?

d. Make a plan by which this hypothesis can be tested to see if it is the answer (or a plausible explanation) in light of the kind of experiments which you can do.

e. Do the experiment which, according to your evaluation in step #d, will test your hypothesis. (Include controls.)

f. Record carefully the data which is generated from the experiment. Record the equipment and procedures which were used so that same experiment can be duplicated, using your instructions, by another investigator.

g. Evaluate the data from the experiment and decide if it proved the hypothesis which you established to test for an answer to your question or problem. If so, the "problem" is solved.

# 3. METRIC CONVERSIONS
## (Grades 4-8)

## Temperature Conversion Chart
### Centigrade to Fahrenheit Conversion

| °C | °F | °C | °F | °C | °F | °C | °F |
|----|----|----|----|----|----|----|----|
| 0 | 32 | 26 | 79 | 51 | 124 | 76 | 169 |
| 1 | 34 | 27 | 81 | 52 | 126 | 77 | 171 |
| 2 | 36 | 28 | 82 | 53 | 127 | 78 | 172 |
| 3 | 37 | 29 | 84 | 54 | 129 | 79 | 174 |
| 4 | 39 | 30 | 86 | 55 | 131 | 80 | 176 |
| 5 | 41 | 31 | 88 | 56 | 133 | 81 | 178 |
| 6 | 43 | 32 | 90 | 57 | 135 | 82 | 180 |
| 7 | 45 | 33 | 91 | 58 | 136 | 83 | 181 |
| 8 | 46 | 34 | 93 | 59 | 138 | 84 | 183 |
| 9 | 48 | 35 | 95 | 60 | 140 | 85 | 185 |
| 10 | 50 | 36 | 97 | 61 | 142 | 86 | 187 |
| 11 | 52 | 37 | 99 | 62 | 144 | 87 | 189 |
| 12 | 54 | 38 | 100 | 63 | 145 | 88 | 190 |
| 13 | 55 | 39 | 102 | 64 | 147 | 89 | 192 |
| 14 | 57 | 40 | 104 | 65 | 149 | 90 | 194 |
| 15 | 59 | 41 | 106 | 66 | 151 | 91 | 196 |
| 16 | 61 | 42 | 108 | 67 | 153 | 92 | 198 |
| 17 | 63 | 43 | 109 | 68 | 154 | 93 | 199 |
| 18 | 64 | 44 | 111 | 69 | 156 | 94 | 201 |
| 19 | 66 | 45 | 113 | 70 | 158 | 95 | 203 |
| 20 | 68 | 46 | 115 | 71 | 160 | 96 | 205 |
| 21 | 70 | 47 | 117 | 72 | 162 | 97 | 207 |
| 22 | 72 | 48 | 118 | 73 | 163 | 98 | 208 |
| 23 | 73 | 49 | 120 | 74 | 165 | 99 | 210 |
| 24 | 75 | 50 | 122 | 75 | 167 | 100 | 212 |
| 25 | 77 | | | | | | |

## Temperature Conversion Formula
Fahrenheit to Centigrade: $C° = 5/9 \times (F° -32)$
Centigrade to Fahrenheit: $F° = (9/5 \times C°) +32$

Weight Conversions

1 gram = .035 ounces
1 kilogram = 2.2 pounds
1 ounce = 28.3 grams
1 pound = 454 grams

Length Conversions

1 micron = 1/1,000 millimeter or 1/25,400 inch
1,000 millimeters = 1 meter
1 centimeter = .3937 inch
1 meter = 3.28 feet; 39.37 inches
1 inch = 2.54 centimeters
1 foot = 30.48 centimeters

Volume Conversions

1 cubic centimeter = 1 milliliter (water at 4° C)
1,000 milliliters = 1 liter
1 liter = 1.05 liquid quarts
1 U.S. fluid ounce = 29.33 milliliters
1 teaspoon = 5 cubic centimeters

## 4. PAPER AIRPLANES AND KITES
## (Grades 4-8)

To study the air and its behavior, flight, etc., excellent lessons can be built around paper airplanes and kites. Students can consult science books and encyclopedias to learn some of the principles of flight. To design and build a kite makes a good science lesson. The test is simply whether or not it will fly.

Many designs can be used in devising paper airplanes. The designs shown in the illustration can be used easily to show the effect of fins. Make a plane, such as the one in the illustration. Fold the tips down, and the plane flies down. Fold one up and one down and, of course, it flies in a spiral. Many more ideas can be developed from such a simple teaching tool.

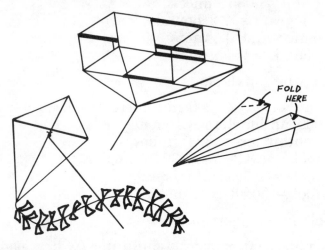

## 5. DETERMINING DIRECTIONS
(Grades 4-8)

It is easy to use a wrist watch as a compass on a day when the sun is visible. To do so, point the hour hand (it must be standard time for your zone — so, if you are on daylight saving time, **mentally move** the hour hand one hour slower) in the direction the sun is. **Halfway between** that line and 12 is **south.** West, then, would be to the right, east to the left and north behind.

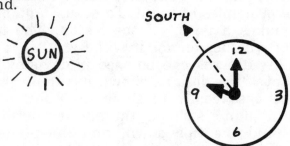

# 6. PLANTS IN THE CLASSROOM (Grades 4-8)

## A. Germinating seeds:

Obtaining seeds is often a problem. Do not overlook such sources as dry Lima and soup beans from the supermarket, garden seeds which students may find at home, birdseed (a mixture of weed seeds) and weed seeds which students can collect locally in vacant lots or around the school grounds. Such "seed containers" as burrs and stick-tights can often be collected from weed stalks even in winter. Seed heads from most weeds can serve as a source of seed germination materials.

For successful seed germination, the seeds must be kept constantly moist once germination has begun. Temperature and absence of light do have some effect also. To hasten germination, soak the seeds for a few hours (or overnight) to soften the seed coat. Then, place seeds in cups with wet paper or in soil. Some seeds may take 2 to 3 weeks for germination. Others like radishes may germinate in 1 to 2 days, depending on the temperature (temperatures from 75-85° F hasten germination of radishes). The half-pint milk cartons, rinsed, are adequate for germination and growing experiments. Paper towels can be used instead of soil.

## B. Keeping plants:

A wide variety of house plants can be kept successfully in the regular classroom. Adequate light and moisture are the only requirements for most of them. If there are any questions about particular plants, it is advised that you ask a local florist for advice.

If you anticipate occasional need to pot plants, it is cheaper to collect woods or garden soil and keep a box of it in the classroom. Place the soil in a large plastic bag, such as a garbage bag, and place that in the box. Avoid soil which is mostly sand or clay. If the soil seems to pack together easily, not being loose, mix a handful of decaying leaf materials collected in a woods or some peat moss in a portion of the soil before putting it in the pot. This permits easy drainage and air space within the soil.

During vacations, to provide water for the plants, stand them in a tray in which an inch or so of water can be held. The water will be absorbed by the plants through the opening in the bottom of the pot and move up through the soil keeping the roots well watered.

In the fall, before frosts occur, a good source of plants is the garden or flower garden. Plants, such as Begonia and Coleus, are widely planted in flower gardens and grow well indoors, too.

For pots, any containers in which a hole can be made in the bottom to permit drainage serve well, e.g., paper and plastic containers as well as standard clay or plastic pots. Various types of hanging baskets made from wire, such as hardware cloth, work well in a classroom where there is limited surface space.

### C. Transpiration—Water Loss by Plants

To demonstrate that plants give off water, select a plant, such as a geranium, for use. Water it and cover the soil around the plant with aluminum foil to prevent water from the soil from evaporating into the plastic bag. Then, cover the plant with a clear plastic bag. Choose a bag which is large enough to cover the plant and extend down over the edge of the pot, as shown in the illustration. Place the plant on the window sill and observe it for a few days. Water droplets will be seen on the plastic.

Another method for checking water loss from leaves is to use a piece of cobalt chloride paper. (Mix the cobalt chloride using about 1 teaspoon of it to about 18 teaspoons of water. Soak the paper or paint the surface of the paper with the solution.) This paper turns pink when it becomes moist. Use a piece of paper which is large enough to fold over the edge of the leaf so that both the upper and lower surfaces of the leaf are partly covered by it. Hold the paper in place by using a paper clip. Notice that the lower surface will become pink, from water given off by the leaf.

### D. Preserving Plants:

Two methods of preserving plants for classroom use are used widely: drying methods and the wax paper method. To obtain good dried specimens, the plants must be dried quickly to retain as much color as possible and dried under pressure to prevent wrinkling. After the plants are collected, let them wilt for an hour so they are easily arranged on a sheet of newspaper without breaking the plant parts. Arrange the plant on a half sheet of newspaper; slide this paper between sheets of corrugated cardboard. Do the next plant or group of small plants the same way. Stack the "sandwiches" of paper, plant and cardboard. Place a weight, such as books or even a cement block, to provide pressure that prevents wrinkling. Place the stack near a heat source, or in the sun, for rapid drying. To increase drying of specimens, it helps to add a large blotter to either side of the newspaper before the cardboard is added. The wax paper method is simpler. Place the leaves, or entire small plants between sheets of waxed paper. Place a sheet of typing paper on top and use a warm iron to dry the plant and melt wax from the paper. This seals the plant specimen between the sheets of waxed paper. (The sheet of typing paper prevents the waxed paper from sticking to the iron.)

## 7. GROWING MICROSCOPIC PLANTS AND ANIMALS (Grades 4-8)

If a microscope or a microprojector is available, it is useful to study collected and cultured organisms.

Algae are the simplest green plants. To prepare a solution for maintaining them in the classroom, place a tablespoon of garden soil in a quart of water and boil for ten minutes. When it has cooled, strain and use that water for the algae. Cladophora is one form of algae very commonly found in aquariums. Euglena is collected in pond water frequently. To see it, one must use a magnification of at least 100 diameters. Keep these green plants in the light. Any transparent container will do. Cover the jar to prevent evaporation. Yeast which is used in baking is a simple plant, a relative of the algae, but with no chlorophyll. It, therefore, must get its food from other sources. It lives on sugar and similar chemicals. Obtain either cake or dry yeast. To observe the plants, they must be magnified at least 100 diameters. Dissolve some yeast in water and add half a teaspoon of sugar per glass of water (use a "pinch" of yeast). If students can see the yeast as soon as it dissolved, they will see round cells, looking like little balls. As the yeast grows, it starts to reproduce by budding. See the illustration below. A small bump appears on the side of the yeast cell. The bud grows until it is as large as the parent cell and then breaks away. The yeast grows rapidly, using the sugar as food and gives off carbon dioxide. The carbon dioxide is what causes the bread to rise. This gas escapes through the dough causing the rising. To illustrate the impact of yeast, mix some flour, water and sugar into dough. In one ball of dough, add 1/4 teaspoon of yeast, made into a

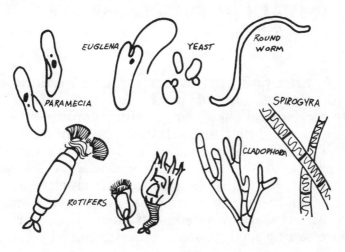

paste. Work it well through the dough. To the other balls of dough, add one teaspoon of yeast and two teaspoons of yeast. Watch the difference in rising. Microscopic animals can be grown or collected from local ponds. Paramecium is a very common protozoan, a one-celled animal. To culture this animal, boil some tap water for 5 minutes and let it cool. Into a quart of water, place a handful of dry grass collected from a vacant lot or park. The grass will probably have on its surface the reproductive structures of Paramecium. In a week, the animals can be seen if the water is examined under the microscope.

By collecting plant materials and water from local ponds, other animals, such as rotifers and roundworms, are found. They can be kept in the water in which they were collected or placed in an aquarium. To a quart of water, add about 3 grains of cooked rice to serve as a food source for bacteria. The bacteria will multiply rapidly and serve as a food source for the other microscopic animals.

## 8. ANIMALS IN THE CLASSROOM
(Grades 4-8)

### A. Earthworms

A colony of earthworms can be maintained with a minimum of work. For a container, a plastic wastebasket or similar container will serve well. Fill the container three-fourths full with soil. Do not use sandy soil since the sand is injurious to the gut of the worm. Mix the soil with the decaying leaf material which can be collected in any wooded area. Add earthworms. In an average wastebasket keep 12-25, or so, worms. For feed, place a small handful of cornmeal, sometimes mixed with coffee grounds, in one corner of the box. Use the same corner each time so the worms will gather there and be easier to collect. Cover the soil with wet burlap or other coarse cloth which can be kept moist. The soil should be moist, not wet. Collect worms for the colony in a field or park on a rainy night or obtain from a bait supply store. Some stores, in the sport or pet department, sell a material for maintaining earthworms. It can be used in place of soil. Feed the worms twice weekly and check to be certain that the soil is moist. (Grass and shredded lettuce can be buried in the soil occasionally.)

## B. Insects

Of the million and a half kinds of animals in the world, more than 600,000 kinds are insects. They provide excellent organisms for study of live animals.

Crickets and grasshoppers are easily kept in jars or screen cages. Feed them dry dog food, lettuce and water. Water can be kept in a small dish. By warming and cooling these insects, it is easy for students to observe changes in behavior. Place some of them in a jar in a refrigerator (or cooler with ice) for 15-30 minutes. Then observe their behavior. They will be sluggish. Then, place them under a lamp or in the sunlight to warm them. Movement becomes much more rapid.

Cocoons are fascinating to watch in class. If students bring cocoons to class, place the cocoon in a container with some soil in it. Suspend the cocoon on a twig or thread so that it does not touch the moist soil and get moldy. Cover the jar with cheese cloth or a screen. Keep the soil moist. When the adult emerges from the cocoon, place a cotton ball soaked in sugar water in the jar so it can eat. Cocoons are made of silk and are the pupa cases of moths. Butterflies pass through their pupa stage in a chrysalis which is a plastic-like structure. Moths have feathery antennae. Butterflies, golf-club-like antennae.

## C. Mealworms

The mealworm is the larva stage of a beetle. It is an excellent animal with which to demonstrate complete metamorphosis (egg, larva, pupa, adult). These worms are available from many pet stores and from scientific supply houses. Place the worms in a container; such as, a plastic wastebasket, glass jar or wooden box. (Cardboard is not good since the worms can chew through it.) Fill the container one-half to three-fourths full with bran, oatmeal or other cereal. For moisture, add peels from potatoes, apples, etc., or wet paper towels. Water poured into the meal causes mold and will destroy the colony. The worm is the larva. The pupa is a beetle-shaped white creature. The adult is a brown beetle. Eggs are laid by the adult females. If it is available, cover the surface with burlap or other coarse cloth. The larvae rub against this to help shed their skins as they grow.

## D. Crayfish or crawdads

These crustaceans, collected in local streams and ponds or obtained from bait dealers, are best kept in a tray with a couple of inches of water. A few stones under which they can hide should be added. Feed them lettuce or meat for fish food.

## E. Fish

In an aquarium, both tropical fish and fish caught locally can be kept. Excellent fish foods include crushed dry dog food and dry oatmeal.

## F. Amphibians

Frogs and toads, often brought to class by students, can be kept in gallon jars or terraria. A tray of water should be provided so they do not dry out. Since these animals do rely on their moist skin to absorb some of their oxygen, it is essential that they be kept moist. Feed them insects, small earthworms or mealworms.

Salamanders and newts are also amphibians and must be kept moist. Newts can be kept in an aquarium with fish.

## G. Tadpoles

Frog larvae are tadpoles. They can be collected in ponds all year. Bullfrog tadpoles live in ponds for at least a year before developing into a frog. In the fall, winter and spring tadpoles can usually be found (if there are frogs in the pond at all) by scraping a net over the bottom debris in a pond. Tadpoles can also be purchased in many pet stores and from scientific supply houses. Tadpoles can be placed in an aquarium with fish or kept by themselves. Feed them boiled lettuce, hard boiled egg yolk, or fish food. They will also eat aquarium plants. As the front legs develop, the animal has developed to the point where it is using its lungs for much of its "breathing." Therefore, at that time, add a piece of wood as a raft (or a piece of styrofoam) so that the animal may rest on it. When the legs are all well developed and the tail is barely obvious, place the frog in a terrarium, or a container with a dish of water so it can be mostly on dry surface. It will then be a "meat eater" and require worms, insects, etc.

## H. Mammals

Mammals are hair-bearing animals. In the classroom often such mammals as gerbils, hamsters, guinea pigs and rabbits are kept. Of these, **gerbils** are most easily maintained since they do not produce a strong urine smell. Their cages need not be changed more often than every 2 or 3 weeks. Use cedar chips on the floor. For feed use a mixture of equal parts of sunflower seeds, birdseed and dry dog food. The mixture can be fed to all of the mammals, with a supplement occasionally of lettuce, carrots, etc. **Hamsters** are often more nervous than gerbils or guinea pigs and less easily handled. Hamsters cages should be cleaned every few days. Use cedar chips on the floor. **Guinea pigs** are easily handled and make good classroom pets. Their cages should be changed every few days. Use cedar chips on the floor of the cage. **Rabbits** can be exciting classroom pets, but must have their cages cleaned daily. Newspaper is a good covering for the floor. Besides the dry food mixture, feed them various fresh vegetables.

Observing animals in class can be done by placing the animal in a jar or box so it can be seen by a small group or the entire class. Smaller animals, such as worms, insects and fish, can be often more easily observed in outline form on a screen. Place the animal in a transparent tray such as a baking dish or plastic button box on the overhead projector.

Movement of legs and the entire body can be seen by the entire class.

## 9. SET-UPS (Grades 4-8)

### A. Ant Colony

Observing the activities of an ant colony provides another way of seeing behavior of live animals. The container should be a gallon glass jar. In the center of the jar stand a #10 tin can, a jar with a lid or a block of wood to act as a spacer. The soil then is sprinkled around the center spacer. In this way the ants must stay closer to the glass as they build their tunnels. Find an ant hill in a field or lot. Using a trowel or shovel, remove the top layer and dig down to where the ants are living. Then, shovel that soil and ants into the jar. If you do not get the queen (a much larger individual) the colony will die off in a few weeks, but that is not a great problem. For food, feed the ants bread and jelly,

meat, raw vegetables, etc. A wet sponge on top will provide water. Keep it moist. Place the lid on the jar and with a small nail or tack make a half dozen small holes in the center of the lid. On the underside of the lid, place a ring of vaseline around the holes so the ants will not get out. Or, set the jar in a tray of water to contain any ants which do escape from the jar. Cover the jar with aluminum foil when no one is observing it, or the ants will work into the soil to avoid the light. Occasionally, shake it up so they have tunnels to rebuild.

## B. Aquarium

One of the best teaching aids is an aquarium. It provides a focus for animal behavior, environments and just fascination for life. The container can be a standard aquarium or a glass jar. Although one can be set up in a gallon, or even a quart jar, it is better to have at least a 10-gallon tank. Gravel provides a hiding place for some animals and rooting anchor for plants. Use about a pound of gravel per gallon of water. If there will be no filter in the tank, slope the gravel toward the front. Then, weekly, using a basting brush or substitute, the gravel can be "swept" pushing the debris which may have accumulated such as left-over food, down against the glass into the "groove" at the bottom of the gravel slope. In this way waste materials can be pushed into a corner and easily removed. Plant plants to suit your own taste. In selecting plants, it is best to seek advice of a local aquarium store operator — and use prices as a guide. Plants, contrary to popular belief, do not contribute measurably to aerating the water. They serve primarily as decoration, hiding places and food for the fish, snails, etc. Water should be drawn from the tap and stand in the tank, or open jars, for several hours, preferably overnight, to aerate. This permits a loss of chemicals used in treating the water. Also, and just as important, the temperature rises to room temperature. Selecting fish again can be done by personal preference and price. In a tank, the "rule of thumb" for population is one inch of fish (measured tip of nose to base of tail, not including the tail) per gallon of water. If you use an air pump, this rule need not be followed so carefully. Be certain that the table on which the tank is placed will support its weight. Gravel, tank and water (8½ pounds per gallon) may totally weigh 100 to 200 pounds. Other animals besides fish can include snails, clams, newt and tadpoles. For food, use dry dog food or oatmeal as well as the commercial fish foods. DO NOT overfeed. Once the tank population is set, determine how much food to give in this way: pour out a pile of food the size of a quarter and keep feeding for five minutes, adding food as soon as all on the water is eaten. After five minutes, determine how much was consumed. Feed that amount every day or so. No more.

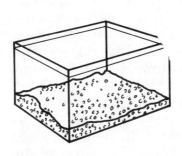

To protect the plants from being completely eaten by snails, add a piece of lettuce (about 3 inches square) weekly. Boil the lettuce so it is softened for the snails. After a couple of hours, remove any lettuce remaining. Tadpoles will also eat lettuce. Each tadpole will eat a square of lettuce weekly.

Never move an aquarium when it is filled. There is too much of a chance that the seams will be strained and develop leaks. Drain the tank to below a quarter level before trying to lift it.

## C. Terrarium

A terrarium is a dry land environment. For example, it can be desert, woodland or swamp. A container may be a bottle, jug, or aquarium tank. On the bottom, place some gravel in which there is some charcoal, a small handful for a 5-gallon tank. The charcoal will prevent souring of water which stands in the gravel, if any. On top of that layer add a layer of peat moss or crushed leaves to keep the soil from getting into the gravel. Then, add soil. If the tank is big enough, add two to three inches of soil or sand; otherwise, a sprinkling is sufficient to hold plants. For plants, if it is possible to get mosses, ferns, etc., from nearby wooded areas, this is best. Also, from a wooded area, decaying wood can be found. Insects, centipedes and other woodland animals may be found to add to the terrarium, as well as land snails. For a "pond" in the tank, it is cleaner to add a dish or aluminum tray — small — burying it so it is level with the soil. When the water needs changing, the dish can be removed and cleaned easily and replaced. Toads, frogs, various insects, snails and lizards are examples of animals which live well in terraria. Feed them weekly and remove uneaten food after a few hours. To make a terrarium in a jug or bottle, bend a wire, such as that from a coat hanger, into a hook and use that to place plants, level soil, etc. Water to keep the soil moist, not wet. To reduce mold growth, add a sprinkling of powdered sulpher which can be purchased from a local druggist.

In desert terraria, cacti can be planted by burying the small pots in which they come. Then, rearranging is easier on the plants. This can also be done in other types of terraria in which potted plants may be used.

### D. A Bird Bath

**Materials:** A large flower pot saucer and a few pebbles to put in the bottom of it; a pole about 3 inches in diameter and four feet high; a small amount of cement.

**Procedure:** Sink the pole into the ground and fill in around it with cement to make it solid. Bolt the saucer to the top of the pole through the center hole. Fill the bottom of the saucer around the hole with cement and smooth down.

### E. Bird Houses that are Different

1. An easy way to make a bird house is by using an old straw hat. Most families have an old straw hat that they no longer use. If not, they can be bought at a rummage sale or a re-sale shop.

Tack the hat on a board that is large enough to hold the hat with an inch or two of board left over on all sides. Tack it securely around the brim edge. Cut a hole in the center of the crown of the hat just large enough for the kind of bird that you wish to attract. Punch three small holes in the bottom of the hat, where the brim is attached to the crown, to allow for drainage. Hang it in a tree and watch the birds nest.

2. A pop bottle carton can be used for a bird house by adding a wooden roof. A piece of tin bent to fit the top of the carton makes a fine roof.

A carton of this type can also be used to make churches or other buildings by adding a roof of construction paper, cutting windows, and painting the carton.

### F. Bird Feeders

1. A board with a one inch frame around it to keep the food from blowing off may be suspended from a branch of a tree by wires fastened at each corner and joined at the top to loop over a branch.

2. Birds like feeders made of natural things, and pine cones are very attractive to them. Mix dry cereal, cracker crumbs, seeds, etc., with peanut butter. Press the mixture into the openings of the pine cone. Wrap a wire around the top of the cone and fasten it onto a branch of a tree. Use a large cone to keep from having to refill it too often. Birds will flock around the filled cone.

## 10. STUDYING ANIMALS BEHAVIOR WITH THE OVERHEAD PROJECTOR (Grades 4-8)

The behavior of small animals can be easily observed by the whole class through the use of the overhead projector. As the cartoon crayfish in the illustration shows, a tray such as a baking dish or transparent plastic box will serve well. Use fish, to observe the use of fins and general body activity. Use salamanders to show use of legs.

One of the best demonstrations is to use a crayfish. Place it in a tray with some water. Feed it pieces of lunch meat, bread, lettuce, etc. The action of its eating will be in outline on the screen for all to see.

# * 11. MEASURING CALORIES
## (Grades 4-8)

A calorie is a unit of heat given off when a fuel, such as our food, is burned. One way to illustrate this well is to make a simple calorimeter such as that shown in the illustration. Here a flask of water, with a **measured** amount of water, is placed on a ring stand or other support. Around the base of the flask make a protective shield from asbestos pads or aluminum foil. This shield will prevent heat loss. The amount of heat given off in the experiment is calculated by determining how much the water temperature rises. A calorie is defined as the amount of heat required to raise the temperature of 1 cc. of water by one degree. Therefore, it is necessary to know exactly how many cc's of water one has and what the original temperature of the water was, i.e., before heating began. To provide the source of heat, use the meat from a walnut (or peanut). Spear the nut meat on a dissecting needle to

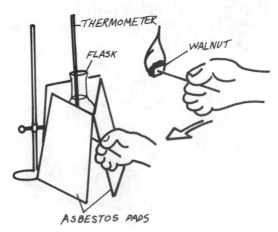

THERMOMETER

FLASK

WALNUT

ASBESTOS PADS

*This activity is available in Inquire Volume I of the **Spice**™ Duplicating Masters.

hold it easily. Then, light the nut meat with a match. Place the burning nut under the flask of water in the shield. As soon as the nut is burned, stir the water with the thermometer and take the temperature reading. Then, the calorie content of the nut can be determined.

## 12. FIELD TRIPS WITH A THEME
## (Grades 4-8)

Field trips have many functions. Some are closely tied to classroom work; others are more for fun. From all of the trips, a far greater benefit will be gained if a theme is defined.

When students are taken to the zoo on a trip, for example, there are many animals and behaviors to observe. Even the accomplished and well-organized student has a problem getting the most from such a trip. To make the experience a real learning experience, choose a theme for the zoo trip. A good theme is animal appendages (feet, especially). Instruct students to study the feet, their shape, size, etc., and to note also in what kind of a native environment the animal lives. Even the use of binoculars can help here, to permit students to get a close look at the feet. Sketches can be made, or photos taken when possible.

Such a theme ties together the observing which students will do and they can carry the theme from one animal to the next and have a point of comparison. Do instruct the students to look at as much of the animal as they wish, but note the appendages and their use. In seals, the flippers; in birds, the wings; in snakes, the abscence of appendages; in elephants, the massive feet; in deer the delicate feet, etc.

This same theme can be developed for the aquarium where shape, placement and use of fins of fish can be studied. In the natural history museum, similar plans can be built around the dioramas. Often, studying the museum dioramas first to see feet close up and still is a good motivation for seeing the feet "in action" on the living animal at the zoo.

Themes relating to ecological adaptations, shape and size of animals, nature and coloring of body cover, i.e., hair, scales, etc., are other points to be considered.

Using this approach to a field trip, whether in a zoo or a museum or out in the woods, the students have a point of focus which helps them to organize their own observations and thinking as they work on the field trip.

## 13. COMMON ANIMAL AND PLANT GROUPS — A SUMMARY (Grades 4-8)

Phylum Protozoa — one celled animals. About 20,000 species.

EUGLENA    AMOEBA    PARAMECIUM

PROTOZOA

Phylum Porifera — body wall with canals. About 5,000 species.

PORIFERA

BATH SPONGE

VENUS'S FLOWER BASKET

Phylum Coelenterata — hollow body, with stinging shells, tentacles. About 10,000 species.

SEA ANEMONE

JELLY FISH

COELENTERATA

Phylum Platyhelminthes — flat worms with only one opening in digestive system. About 10,000 species.

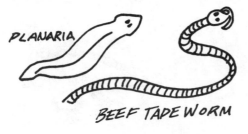

PLANARIA

BEEF TAPE WORM

PLATYHELMINTHES

Phylum Nematoda — roundworms, digestive tube with both mouth and anus. About 10,000 species.

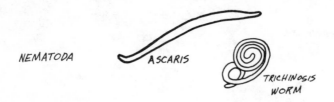

Phylum Mollusca — soft-bodied animals, often with shell produced by organ called mantle. About 80,000 species.

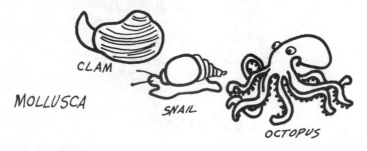

Phylum Annelida — segmented worms, with main nerve cord on lower side. About 6,200 species.

Phylum Arthropoda — jointed appendages, body covered with hard exoskeleton. About 940,000 species.

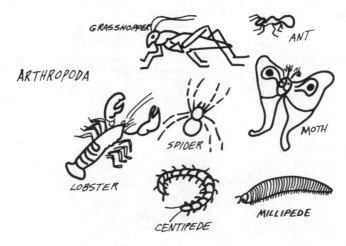

Phylum Echinodermata — spiny-skinned, with water vascular system, tube feet. About 5,600 species.

Phylum Chordata, subphylum Vertebrata backbone, sense organs in head, red blood, internal bony skeleton. About 40,000 species.

Fish — appendages are fins, breathe by gills, scales on skin. Cold blooded. About 30,000 species.

FISH          PERCH

Amphibia — double life, tadpole which is aquatic; adult, usually terrestrial, skin naked, moist, cold blooded. About 3,000 species.

AMPHIBIA          FROG

Reptiles — both young and adults air-breathing skin with scales, dry, claws on feet, if present, cold-blooded. About 6,000 species.

REPTILES          BOX TURTLE

Birds — body covered with feathers, front appendages are wings, legs with scales, warm blooded. About 8,700 species.

BIRDS  ALBATROSS

Mammals — body covered with hair, young fed on milk secreted from mother, warm blooded. About 3,500 species.

MAMMALS  RAT

Phylum Thallophyta — plants with no roots, stems or leaves; plant body a thallus; algae have chlorophyll, fungi do not. Algae — about 20,000 species. Fungi — about 80,000 species.

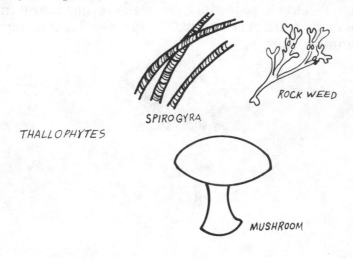

THALLOPHYTES

SPIROGYRA

ROCK WEED

MUSHROOM

Phylum Bryophyta — plants with simple stems and leaves, no roots. About 25,000 species.

BRYOPHYTES

STAR MOSS  LIVERWORT

Phylum Pteridophyta — plants with roots, stems, leaves, reproduce by spores. About 10,000 species.

PTERIDOPHYTES

FERN

Phylum Spermatophyta — plants with roots, stems, leaves, reproduce by seeds either borne in cones or fruit. About 200,000 species. Most of our common plants.

SPRUCE

SPERMATOPHYTES

PALM

# INDEX

FOR TEACHER NOTES

FOR TEACHER NOTES

**FOR TEACHER NOTES**

FOR TEACHER NOTES

FOR TEACHER NOTES

# DRAMA-PAK™

Each "Pak" contains a playbook for each main character and one for the director.

## SCHOOL FOR ANGELS
### A Fantasy · by Natalie Bovee Hutson
### Six Main Characters

Less than one week until Christmas and chaos reigns in The Great Beyond! While Earth bombards the Heavenly Headmaster with urgent requests for "perfect" angels, it is discovered that the current "crop" is woefully lacking in "angel skills". Cherubs have been playing frisbee with the stars, conducting pillow fights with the clouds, and swinging from the Pearly Gates. The angel choir doesn't even know the words to "Silent Night"!

A delightful play for all ages and all seasons.

☐  304-7...................................................$9.95

## THE GRUMBLE GROUP
### A Comedy · by Natalie Bovee Hutson
### Five Characters

The Grumble Group meets regularly (and grudgingly) at a city bus stop, where they find endless subjects about which to complain. On the surface these four individuals appear to be cantankerous old-timers, finding nothing right with the world. But as they reveal themselves to the audience, and through the help of an optimistic newcomer, it slowly becomes apparent that beneath the somewhat comic exteriors, lie sensitive people who have, for various reasons, become quite disenchanted with life.

A good choice for all ages.

☐  301-2...................................................$9.95

## ME, BETH CONNORS
### A Teenage Drama · by Natalie Bovee Hutson
### Seven Characters

Meet Beth Connors, an average twelve-year-old, who through a series of flashbacks, takes the audience by the hand and leads them through a typical day in her life. It's a day filled with girlish giggling, a mysterious phone call, and the usual scraps with a pesky younger brother. But best of all, it is a day in which a routine visit to her grandmother in a nursing home, enables Beth to view life in a more adult manner.

☐  303-9...................................................$9.95

# DRAMA-PAK™

Each "Pak" contains a playbook for each main characters and one for the director.

## MR. TEDLEY'S TREEHOUSE
### A Drama for the Young · by Natalie Bovee Hutson
### Seven Characters

Mr. Tedley is a child's dream come true. He lives alone in a treehouse surviving on berries and nuts, offering friendship and vast knowledge to the younger set. But is he real? Ryan and Joey know that he is, but cannot convince others of the fact, and this troubles them.

In a simplistic way, the play deals with every child's need to fantasize and cling to dreams. Yet it also emphasizes that there comes a time when one must leave the fantasies behind and face the real world.

A charming play for young and old.

☐  302-0.................................................$9.95

## THE READING OF THE WILL
### A Farce · by Natalie Bovee Hutson
### Seven Characters

Henry P. Jaybody may be deceased, but he is not absent from the reading of his will! Knowing that his greedy heirs would do their best to "out-mourn" each other, Henry had the foresight to plan a scene which would send the tribe in all directions, showing their true colors - and practically trampling one another in the process.

An action-filled play with characters who are fun to portray and even funnier to watch.

☐  305-5.................................................$9.95

## THE WRONGFUL CLAIM
### An Old-Fashioned Melodrama · by Natalie Bovee Hutson
### Eight Characters

The lovely and innocent Melody Lark is but a servant in the home of wealthy Vanessa Vapors. Vanessa's avaricious daughter, Crystal, is envious of Melody's childlike charm and attentions of the gardener, Barnaby Barnhart. So when Crystal accidentally discovers that Melody is about to fall heir to a fortune, she plots her disinheritance. Unaware of his sister's scheme, an equally greedy Humphrey Vapors devises his own plot to discredit Melody.

An old-fashioned melodrama with lots of heroes and villains and a chance to hiss, boo, and applaud them all.

☐  300-4.................................................$9.95

# DUPLICATOR BOOKS

Use our ideas in duplicator form to cut teacher preparation time and fulfill the needs for supplementary activities in the following areas of study:

### LANGUAGE ARTS

☐ **ED501-5 SPICE VOL. I** — K-2
☐ **ED502-3 SPICE VOL. II** — 2-4
☐ **ED505-8 ANCHOR VOL. I** — 4-6
☐ **ED506-6 ANCHOR VOL. II** — 6-8
☐ **ED564-3 PHONICS VOL. I** — K-2
☐ **ED565-1 PHONICS VOL. II** — 2-4
☐ **ED567-8 GRAMMAR VOL. I** — 4-6
☐ **ED568-6 GRAMMAR VOL. II** — 6-8
☐ **ED509-0 RESCUE VOL. I** — K-4
   (Remedial Reading)
☐ **ED516-3 FLAIR VOL. I** — 3-8
   (Creative Writing)
☐ **ED527-9 DICTIONARY VOL. I** — K-2
   (Single Letters)
☐ **ED528-7 DICTIONARY VOL. II** — K-2
   (Blends)
☐ **ED529-5 DICTIONARY VOL. III** — 3-6
☐ **ED530-9 DICTIONARY VOL. IV** — 7-9
☐ **ED537-6 LIBRARY VOL. I** — 3-6
☐ **ED538-4 LIBRARY VOL. II** — 7-9

### MUSIC

☐ **ED561-9 NOTE VOL. I** — K-2
☐ **ED562-7 NOTE VOL. II** — 3-6

### SAFETY

☐ **ED519-8 PREVENT VOL. I** — K-4
☐ **ED520-1 PREVENT VOL. II** — 4-8

### ONLY
## $6.95 Each

### EARLY LEARNING

☐ **ED512-0 LAUNCH VOL. I**
   (Basic Readiness)
☐ **ED513-9 LAUNCH VOL. II**
   (Additional Skills)

### MATHEMATICS

☐ **ED533-3 PLUS VOL. I** — K-2
☐ **ED534-1 PLUS VOL. II** — 2-4
☐ **ED523-6 CHALLENGE VOL. I** — 4-6
☐ **ED524-4 CHALLENGE VOL. II** — 6-8

### SCIENCE

☐ **ED546-5 PROBE VOL. I** — K-2
☐ **ED547-3 PROBE VOL. II** — 2-4
☐ **ED550-3 INQUIRE VOL. I** — 4-8

### SOCIAL STUDIES

☐ **ED553-8 SPARK VOL. I** — K-2
☐ **ED554-6 SPARK VOL. II** — 2-4
☐ **ED557-0 FOCUS VOL. I** — 4-6
☐ **ED558-9 FOCUS VOL. II** — 6-8

* * * * * * * * * * * * * * * * * * * * * * * * * * * * * * * * * * * * *

### ONLY
## $4.50 Each

**EXCLUSIVE WORD LISTS**
Each book contains a graded word list — from 738 words at Level 1 to 4,325 words at Level 6.

# "Work with Words" Duplicator Books Develop and Reinforce Language Skills on 6 Levels!

A creative new series from the publishers of Spice! Here's a fresh and dynamic approach to teaching and reinforcing language skills. Each master is clearly identified as to the learning objective: recognizing sounds, visual identification, word recognition, word usage, spelling, alphabetizing, word meaning, and so on. Thus the teacher can locate just the right activity at just the right time! To top if off, each book contains our exclusive and previously unpublished graded word list for that level. Each 8½ × 11" book has teacher's guide; 20 masters. Use with any basal program to extend learning through skill-building activities.

☐ **ED262-8** Level 1A — 738 words
☐ **ED263-6** Level 1B — 738 words
☐ **ED264-4** Level 2A — 1416 words
☐ **ED265-2** Level 2B — 1416 words
☐ **ED266-0** Level 3A — 2303 words
☐ **ED267-9** Level 3B — 2303 words
☐ **ED268-7** Level 4A — 2970 words
☐ **ED269-5** Level 4B — 2970 words
☐ **ED270-9** Level 5A — 3613 words
☐ **ED271-7** Level 5B — 3613 words
☐ **ED272-5** Level 6A — 4325 words
☐ **ED273-3** Level 6B — 4325 words
☐ **WWP-500** Complete Set of all 12 books above ............................ $54.00
*Note:* "B" level books are slightly more advanced than "A" level.

Duplicators and idea-books (shown on opposite side) are available at the leading school supply dealers. Ask for them by name.

For a current catalog, contact the publisher.

80484

# IDEA-BOOKS FOR ELEMENTARY SCHOOL TEACHERS

Each book was created to meet teachers' needs for simple and explicit ideas to enrich the many subject areas presented to their students.

**ONLY $6 95 Each**

## LANGUAGE ARTS

☐ **ED101-X SPICE** — Primary Language Arts ● Grades K-4
☐ **ED109-5 ANCHOR** — Intermediate Language Arts ● Grades 4-8
☐ **ED128-1 RESCUE** — Primary Remedial Reading ● Grades K-4
☐ **ED112-5 FLAIR** — Creative Writing ● Grades K-8
☐ **ED122-2 SCRIBE** — Handwriting ● Grades K-8
☐ **ED126-5 PRESS** — Newspaper Activities ● Grades K-8
☐ **ED130-3 PHONICS** — Primary Phonics ● Grades K-4
☐ **ED134-6 GRAMMAR** — Intermediate Grammar ● Grades 4-8
☐ **ED131-1 LISTEN** — Listening Activities ● Grades K-8
☐ **ED133-8 VIDEO** — Television Activities ● Grades K-8
☐ **ED136-2 REFLECT** — Creative Thought ● Grades 4-Adult
☐ **ED137-0 VALUES** — Values Clarification ● Grades K-8

## MATHEMATICS

☐ **ED103-6 PLUS** — Primary Mathematics ● Grades K-4
☐ **ED116-8 CHALLENGE** — Intermediate Mathematics ● Grades 4-8
☐ **ED118-4 METER** — Metrics ● Grades K-8

## SCIENCE

☐ **ED102-8 PROBE** — Primary Science ● Grades K-4
☐ **ED121-4 INQUIRE** — Intermediate Science ● Grades 4-8

## SOCIAL STUDIES

☐ **ED104-4 SPARK** — Primary Social Studies ● Grades K-4
☐ **ED125-7 FOCUS** — Intermediate Social Studies ● Grades 4-8
☐ **ED120-6 CHOICE** — Economics ● Grades K-8
☐ **ED123-0 CAREER** — Career Education ● Grades K-8
☐ **ED135-4 COMPASS** — Map Skills ● Grades K-8

## SPECIALTY STUDIES

☐ **ED111-7 LAUNCH** — Preschool and Kindergarten Readiness
☐ **ED127-3 HOLIDAY** — Holiday Art ● Grades K-8
☐ **ED105-2 CREATE** — Primary Art ● Grades K-4
☐ **ED124-9 CRAFT** — Intermediate Art ● Grades 4-8
☐ **ED113-3 NOTE** — Music ● Grades K-8
☐ **ED119-2 GROWTH** — Health ● Grades K-8
☐ **ED115-X PREVENT** — Safety ● Grades K-8
☐ **ED107-9 STAGE** — Dramatics ● Grades K-8
☐ **ED106-0 ACTION** — Physical Education ● Grades K-6
☐ **ED117-6 DISPLAY** — Bulletin Board Ideas ● Grades K-8

Address: ☐ Home ☐ School (Preferred)

Name _____

Address _____

_____

City _____ State _____ Zip _____

Idea-books and duplicators (shown on the opposite side) are available at leading school supply dealers or Educational Service, Inc., PO Box 219, Stevensville, Michigan 49127 **1-800-253-0763.**

80684